[redacted]

Seven Promises of a Promise Keeper

[redacted]

SEVEN PROMISES OF A PROMISE KEEPER

PUBLISHING
Colorado Springs, Colorado

SEVEN PROMISES OF A PROMISE KEEPER

ISBN 1-56179-293-4

Published by Focus on the Family Publishing, Colorado Springs, CO 80995.

Editors: Al Janssen
Larry K. Weeden

Front Cover Design: David Riley & Associates

Printed in Singapore
94 95 96 97 98/10 9 8 7 6 5 4 3 2 1

Contents

Seize the Moment

by
Randy Phillips
President, The Promise Keepers

The time has come for each of us!

Keith Osborn's moment came as another man at the Promise Keepers conference encouraged him to take the first step in becoming reconciled to his father. Keith had been unable to forgive his dad for the inadequate way he had parented him. "The next morning," Keith said, "all was fine until I went to the restroom at a local restaurant. But then I became convicted by the Holy Spirit and began weeping heavily. I prayed to God and asked what He would have me do, and I was aware that I needed to call my dad as soon as possible. I thought about putting it off and was convicted again to do it right away.

"I found a pay phone, and through the sobbing, I somehow managed to ask my dad to forgive me for the bitterness and anger I had held for him over the previous two years. I explained why I felt this way. He asked me to forgive him as well, *and he told me for the first time in my life that he loved me*. Praise the Lord for this victory!"

For Jerry Smith, his moment came as he listened to Dr. James Dobson talk about what wives need from their husbands—things like romance and taking spiritual leadership in the home. "I needed to hear from other men experiencing the same struggles and searching for a closer relationship with God and direction in their lives," Jerry said after Promise Keepers '93. "I am now committing my wife and son to the Lord first thing every morning on my knees at the foot of my bed. I am watching my words closely, especially toward my wife and child."

Al, a black man, and Joe, a white man, seized a life-changing moment at the end of Promise Keepers '93. As Al was returning to his hotel on Saturday evening after Coach Bill McCartney's closing call for men to work for racial reconciliation, he was approached by Joe. Joe asked if he could speak. When Al said yes, Joe explained that he had grown up in Mississippi hating blacks. Then, with tears in his eyes, he asked Al, "Will you forgive me? And will you help me?"

Al agreed to both requests. And since that night, the two men have stayed in touch. Both are growing in their relationships with Christ and with each other. That's the power of racial reconciliation—and of two men willing to grab an opportunity to do the right thing.

For John, his moment came as he took what he had learned at Promise Keepers '93 home to South Florida. His wife explained: "I told John that he had to go to Promise Keepers somehow. We came up with the money, and he went. He said it was the best thing that had ever happened in his life (after Jesus and me)! And he came home with a vision for other men.

"When he got back, he went to our pastor and began a men's ministry. The men meet on Thursday night every week, and the changes are awesome! The wives will be the first to tell you how things have improved in their homes in every way, including spiritually."

Jerry, Keith, Al, Joe, and John made decisions that will determine the future course of their relationships with God, their families, and their brothers.

They were called to seize the moment!

Why Now?

Just a few years ago, it would have been a minor miracle to get 25 men together at a men's seminar in most churches. Today, however, you find men gathering in hundreds and thousands in almost every city, and they're not just hearing testimonies from famous sports personalities or competing in chili cook-offs. Across the United States and the world men are looking for answers, and they are looking to Jesus to provide them.

In July 1993 in Boulder, Colorado, more than 50,000 men representing every state and every continent met together for Promise Keepers '93. For an entire weekend, they worshiped God in prayer, praise, and song and received teaching on subjects ranging from marriage and child rearing to sexual temptation and accountability. And in the closing challenge, most of those men chose to light their candles as an outward expression of an inner transaction, their commitment to keep the seven promises outlined in this book.

Seeing such an overwhelming response deeply touched me, but it also led me to ask the inevitable question: Why now? Why would men sacrifice the time and effort? Why were so many willing to make such profound commitments to change? What had shifted so much that now men were so open to Jesus? After prayerful consideration, I could reach only one inescapable conclusion: We are at the threshold of a spiritual awakening.

Though the "time of God's favor" has been generously extended to all people in all times through the cross, church historians have noted that there have been specific seasons of God's increased favor throughout history. Scholars use such terms as *outpouring, awakening, movement*, and *revival* to describe those unique periods when God bestows His grace and power in unusual measure upon a people to extend His kingdom on earth. There's a growing consensus among Christian leaders that we are now, once again, in such a time.

This became clear to me in August 1993 when my wife, Holly, and I went to a prayer summit for North American leaders. There, with over 200 other Christian leaders, we honored the person of Jesus during three days of worship and prayer. Having no other agenda than to wait upon God, we set aside our busy schedules and learned to "be still, and know that I am God" (Psa. 46:10).

As the hours turned into days, all of us experienced a profound renewal in the area of God's love for us and the world. While we waited on Him, we were reassured that God "will be exalted among the nations." In that light, I found myself receptive to God's Spirit in a new way that ultimately led me to a larger perspective. I sensed the urgency of God's present call to His church and, more specifically, to His men.

After the final session of the prayer summit, I was surprised by the Lord. That's the only way I can put it. While my wife and I were dining with the chairman of the board of Promise Keepers, Dale Schlafer, and his wife, the Holy Spirit prompted me in a unique and unmistakable way. The words were not audible, but the impression was clear. The sense of the Lord's urging was that we were experiencing a sovereign move of His Spirit to restore the spiritual identity of His sons. Along with that, the biblical injunction to "make the most of every opportunity" was strongly impressed upon my mind. With time, it coalesced into an unshakable directive from the Lord:

We must seize the moment!

As I have talked with Christian leaders across the country, I keep hearing the same refrain: *Carpe Diem!* Seize the day! Seize the God-given opportunity. The Scripture says God will "do immeasurably more than all we ask or imagine, according to his power that is at work within us" (Eph. 3:20). For that to happen, however, we must be men of action, men who are ready to respond by faith to what God has initiated.

As Paul said, we must "be very careful, then, how [we] live—not as unwise but as wise, making the most of every *opportunity*, because the days are evil" (Eph. 5:15-16, emphasis added). Millions of women—wives, mothers, sisters, and daughters—have been praying that the men of the world would respond to the Lord.

I strongly believe those prayers are now being answered. God's Spirit is calling men to rise up! And they are! They're growing into a new and deeper intimacy with Jesus, and through His power they are seizing the spiritual initiative in their homes, churches, friendships, and communities. The responsibilities men have abandoned for too long are once again being vigorously addressed. Men are rising up to become all God originally intended them to be: men of integrity, men who keep their promises.

Kairos

The Greek word for *opportunity* as it appears in the Scriptures is *kairos*. Scholars tell us it means "favorable opportunity." Its derivatives imply "the right moment; that which lasts only for a while." *Kairos* means a God-given opportunity is being offered to mankind at a specific moment in time. However, the word also implies there is a risk—*a risk of faith*. In other words, as time moves on, the opportunity can be missed.

That happened to the Israelites when they failed to enter the Promised Land. God told Moses to "send some men to explore the land of Canaan, which I am giving to the Israelites" (Num. 13:1). So Moses assembled leaders from the 12 tribes and sent them to scout out Canaan and bring back a report.

During the preceding year, those people had witnessed the most spectacular signs of God's favor that any nation could ever hope to see. God humbled

Pharaoh through the various plagues and the Passover. He then parted the waters of the Red Sea and later destroyed the army of Egypt as He closed those same waters. The Israelites had seen God provide water in the desert and had eaten manna, the daily proof that He had not forgotten them. Now God wanted to keep His promise to Abraham and fight for His children as they entered the Promised Land. This was the moment of God's favor.

When the scouts returned from Canaan 40 days later, their report left no doubt in the people's minds that the land was, indeed, very good, "a land flowing with milk and honey." One would think that now they'd rejoice in the goodness of God and seize their land of promise. But they didn't.

Out of fear of their own inadequacies, they doubted the will and power of God to triumph through them. Because of the numerous enemies they had seen, ten of the scouts convinced Israel to turn their backs on this God-given opportunity and return to the relative safety of the desert. In spite of the protests of Moses, Joshua, and Caleb, the people refused God's *kairos*. By failing to seize the moment, they sealed their fate. The window of opportunity slammed shut, and because of it, that entire generation wandered in the desert and perished outside God's will.

God remained faithful, however. The Promised Land would wait until another generation responded in obedience and faith. Those people believed that God's power working through them was greater than the enemy's strength to oppose them. And it was! They conquered the Promised Land and left us a clear lesson.

In the daily course of human events, unique opportunities—*kairous*—to change the destiny of a person or a people appear . . . for a moment. The test of that person or people is whether they will recognize it and respond in obedience to the One who is offering it, trusting in His ability to work through them to fulfill His purposes.

One Man's Response

"What would it be like," Coach McCartney said at Promise Keepers '93, "if a stadium full of men in each state across the country began to take God at His word?" Can you imagine it? What would it be like if hundreds of thousands of men began to seize the moment: with God, with their families, in their churches, and in their communities? Just what would it be like if men were reconciled to God and His will in every area of their lives? What would it be like if they came together based on what they have in common —their love for Jesus? This is the hope of Promise Keepers: that men would dare to enter into the struggle for righteousness and, shoulder to shoulder, seize this divine opportunity to further the kingdom of God.

In 1990, a few men dared to do just that. Coach Bill McCartney and Dr. Dave Wardell asked 70 of their friends to meet together to pray. It was a small beginning. There were no reporters, no fanfare. Just an ordinary group of men with a simple yet profound challenge: "Will you commit to mutual discipleship, reaching out to others, and seeking God's favor for a national revival?"

They'd struck a nerve! Those men were elated by the idea of a movement that would put the focus on men. The time seemed right, and here were two brothers in Christ ready to do something about it. In fact, they wanted to do something that many thought would never happen. They wanted to fill a stadium with men to honor Jesus and to receive training in what it means to be a godly man! Though it represented a significant challenge, those 70 friends and associates soon realized that this was more than just an appeal from a Christian football coach. God had used an ordinary man to bring an appeal from the heart of God to participate in something much bigger than they could ever have imagined. They committed to pray, fast, and plan for a Promise Keepers conference for the men of Colorado.

In July 1991, a year later, 4,200 men showed up, and Promise Keepers was born. In July 1992, 22,000 men came, and a nation looking for hope began to take notice. As men started finding real help for real problems, marriages and families were reconciled, and men refocused on the future of their country—their own children, their churches, and their communities.

Then, in the summer of 1993 in Boulder, Colorado, more than 50,000 men filled the Colorado University football stadium for the express purpose of learning to take God at His word. On hand to help were some of the most noted Bible teachers in the country. When the men were not praising God in song and prayer, they were attending sessions on such subjects as integrity in the marketplace, nurturing family life, and racial reconciliation. God's favor was obvious.

When 50,000 men lifted their voices in a spirit of unity and began to glorify God, something happened. More than 4,000 of them went forward to be reconciled to Jesus Christ. The following night, more than 1,000 pastors went forward, and the stadium erupted in a standing ovation as they chose to be rededicated as the leaders of the church.

Since that conference, we've received thousands of letters telling us how prisoners are being reformed, marriages are being restored, and children are being redeemed. Pastors are writing to tell us how their churches are being renewed. And now, all across the country, men are crossing the socioeconomic, racial, and denominational barriers that have traditionally kept us from being one Body moving in unison under the leadership of Jesus Christ. I believe God is honoring the appeal of the apostle Paul when he said:

> May the God who gives endurance and encouragement give you a spirit of unity among yourselves as you follow Christ Jesus, so that with one heart and mouth you may glorify the God and Father of our Lord Jesus Christ. (Rom. 15:5-6)

In July 1993, men of all colors and denominations sang "Let the Walls Fall Down" and then embraced each other as brothers in Christ. As I watched them, I remembered that this is also what Jesus had prayed for His disciples that last night in the upper room: "May they be brought to complete unity to let the world know that you sent me" (John 17:23). The walls are coming down in a new spirit of unity. Though true reconciliation and mutual accountability will require much more commitment and sacrifice, what we have already seen represents a new beginning, a new hope. Will you join us?

Opportunity

It's a little intimidating to realize that a "time of God's favor" is upon us. For as we've seen, that requires a response. It's doubly intimidating when we see what an impact a few committed men have already had in starting Promise Keepers. Many of us may feel tempted to think that's too great a burden to bear; that our lives, by comparison, are just the routine stuff of paying the bills, trying to please an employer, and building strong marriages and families. But that's just the point—for the vast majority of us, the routines of life are our divinely appointed opportunities. As Paul said:

> "Wake up, O sleeper, rise from the dead, and Christ will shine on you." Be very careful, then, how you live—not as unwise but as wise, making the most of every opportunity, because the days are evil. (Eph. 5:14*b*-16)

Paul warned us—*now* is our personal *kairos*. Like the men of Issachar who "understood the times" (see 1 Chron. 12:32), we are called to understand our times and seize the moment. In Latin, the word *opportunity* means "toward the port." In the ancient world, seamen used it to describe the time when the tide and winds were favorable to make it safely to port. When that moment came, they would set their sails to take full advantage of it. In the same way, when God is at work, as He is now, we must "wake up" to that opportunity, set our sails to His favor, and ride in His boat, using the wind and tide He has created.

How do we do that? Promise Keepers believes it starts by making some promises—promises we intend to keep. That's why we've written *Seven Promises of a Promise Keeper*. These promises emerged out of an intense time of prayer and discussion among our staff and board of directors. Here they are:

1. A Promise Keeper is committed to honoring Jesus Christ through worship, prayer, and obedience to God's Word in the power of the Holy Spirit.

2. A Promise Keeper is committed to pursuing vital relationships with a few other men, understanding that he needs brothers to help him keep his promises.

3. A Promise Keeper is committed to practicing spiritual, moral, ethical, and sexual purity.

4. A Promise Keeper is committed to building strong marriages and families through love, protection, and biblical values.

5. A Promise Keeper is committed to supporting the mission of the church by honoring and praying for his pastor, and by actively giving his time and resources.

6. A Promise Keeper is committed to reaching beyond any racial and denominational barriers to demonstrate the power of biblical unity.

7. A Promise Keeper is committed to influencing his world, being obedient to the Great Commandment (see Mark 12:30-31) and the Great Commission (see Matt. 28:19-20).

As you can see, a Promise Keeper seizes the moment for Jesus by making commitments. Yes, commitments! There is no changing the future without committing to that change. There's no commitment to change when men have a comfortable Christianity that makes no demands on their lives. If we're honest, we must admit that promises have been broken. Relationships have been damaged. And we are out of step with God. It's time for us to rise up and say, "Those days are over!"

These promises are not designed as a new list of commandments to remind us of how badly we're doing with respect to the often-competing demands of the marketplace, the home, and the mission field. Rather, they are meant to guide us toward the life of Christ and to transform us within so that we might see transformation in our homes, among our friends, in our churches, and, ultimately, in our nation.

The time has come! In the final session of Promise Keepers '93, Coach McCartney reminded us all, "We have been *in* a war but not *at* war! If we are to make a difference, it will require much more than we've been doing until now." While we have been asleep in our routines, the enemy has attacked relentlessly, cutting away the spiritual heritage of America. If we don't respond now, time could run out!

When we're in a spiritual war, however, the apostle Paul warned us: "If the trumpet does not sound a clear call, who will get ready for battle?" (1 Cor. 14:8). He's right! We've been too vague with our commitments for too long. There can no longer be any doubt or confusion about what is required. This book is our trumpet call. This book gives us our marching orders!

In the pages to come, we've asked very qualified men, proven warriors, to explain exactly what's required to keep each of the seven promises. Read their words carefully and prayerfully. For even with their clarity to help us, the struggle will be hard; and in it, our character as men will be tested. As C.S. Lewis said, "Courage is not simply one of the virtues, but the form of every virtue at the testing point."

We have also incorporated in the book, after each of the seven promises, a chance for you to personally evaluate your life in light of what you've read. Then we encourage you to work through the book for at least eight weeks in a small group of men—three to five is an ideal number. This will give you a chance to talk about what you've read and to encourage and help one another to implement the commitments you make. A discussion guide is provided for this group use.

Ask God's Spirit to give you the kind of hunger that will produce change. I warn you, this is a powerful process. Twenty-four men from a church in Wichita, Kansas, attended Promise Keepers '92, then formed a men's group that met weekly to encourage and support each other. One of the men had suffered a business failure but seemed to be accepting it well. He had found a new job and appeared to be happy with it. One week, the men viewed Gary

Smalley's video from Promise Keepers '92, "The Man and His Family." Everyone appreciated the message—or so it seemed.

The following night, one of the men, Howard Buhrle, received a call from the wife of the man whose business had failed. She was in tears as she said her husband had just come home and said he was getting a divorce—he just didn't love her anymore, and she would be better off without him.

Howard sprang into action the next day. He contacted the man at work. After some urging, the man agreed to meet with a counselor. "The man and his wife are now meeting with a counselor," Howard reported, "and the Promise Keepers group is paying for the counseling. After the counselor heard what we men were doing, he cut his already low fees another 40 percent. And it looks as though the marriage will be saved."

We believe the Lord is now extending to us His *kairos*, an opportunity to make a difference. But His sons must respond and make the commitments that we believe will seize the moment—the seven promises of a Promise Keeper!

Are You Sure You're a Christian?

You need to do five things to become a part of God's family. If you haven't already done these, I urge you, if you're sincerely ready, to do them now:

1. **Admit** your spiritual need. "I am a sinner."
2. **Repent.** Be willing to turn from your sin and, with God's help, start living to please Him.
3. **Believe** that Jesus Christ died for you on the cross and rose again.
4. **Receive,** through prayer, Jesus Christ into your heart and life. Pray something like this from the sincerity of your heart:

   Dear Lord Jesus,

   I know I am a sinner. I believe You died for my sins and then rose from the grave. Right now, I turn from my sins and open the door of my heart and life. I receive You as my personal Lord and Savior. Thank You for saving me. Amen.

5. Then **tell** a believing friend and a pastor about your commitment.

(Adapted from Greg Laurie, *New Believer's Growth Book* [Riverside, Calif.: Harvest Ministries, 1985], p. 8.)

Seize the Moment
Personal Evaluation

Check the description below that best summarizes your relationship with Jesus right now:

_______ This is the first time I've thought about it.

_______ I've thought about it, but I'm not sure I'm ready to make any decision.

_______ I haven't made a commitment to Christ, but I'm ready to do so.

_______ I think I've made a commitment to Christ, but I'm not sure.

__X__ I know I've made a personal commitment of my life to Christ.

In the Group

In this, your first meeting, take time to get acquainted with each other. The following questions should help you get below the surface.

1. Complete each of the following statements in 60 seconds apiece. (Each member should do this.)

    a) The highlights of my life are . . .
    b) I would characterize my relationship with my father as . . .
    c) One man I greatly admire is MY DAD,
    and the reason is . . .

2. In one minute, tell the group what you would like to see accomplished in your time together over the next eight weeks. (Each member should do this.)

3. Briefly express where you are in your relationship with Jesus Christ. Refer to the personal evaluation above. State which of the five descriptions applies to you and why. (Each member should do this.)

Please note: There should be no pressure to "answer correctly" or to make a decision someone is not ready to make. The purpose of this time is to honestly assess where you are in your relationship with God and help one another move deeper in that relationship. On the other hand, someone in the group may be ready to make a commitment to Christ. The group should encourage that and can pray with him as he asks Jesus into his life.

4. Review the following statements:
   - I agree to be at these meetings for the next eight weeks.
   - I agree to do my best to be honest with you when we meet and discuss the questions at the end of each section of this book.
   - I agree that anything said here remains absolutely confidential.

Are you comfortable with those three commitments? If so, covenant together to faithfully carry them out for each other.

Now get ready to see what God has in store for you!

Memory Verse: "For he [God] says, 'In the time of my favor I heard you, and in the day of salvation I helped you.' I tell you, now is the time of God's favor, now is the day of salvation" (2 Cor. 6:2).

On Your Own

Read the first section of the book, "A Man and His God," before the next meeting.

PROMISE 1

A Man and His God

A Promise Keeper is committed to honoring Jesus Christ through worship, prayer, and obedience to God's Word in the power of the Holy Spirit.

PROMISE 1

Introduction

At the end of His Sermon on the Mount, Jesus said that whoever heard His words and put them into practice was "like a wise man who built his house on the rock. The rain came down, the streams rose, and the winds blew and beat against that house; yet it did not fall, because it had its foundation on the rock" (Matt. 7:24-25).

There's one thing we can be sure of in life—sooner or later, we will endure storms. Many of us have already suffered, or are currently suffering, through difficult times. The issue in this first promise is the foundation on which we rest. We can't avoid the storm, but we can survive it. That's what this first promise is all about—the commitment on which all the other promises rest. It's about our commitment to Jesus Christ.

Three well-equipped men will lead us to a deeper understanding of this promise. Jack Hayford is pastor of The Church on the Way in Van Nuys, California. He has written and composed the music for hundreds of songs, though he is best known for the worship song "Majesty." He will help us see what it means to worship.

Next, Wellington Boone explains why men must pray. Pastor Boone works with churches and national ministries that promote spiritual revival among black youth. His message of prayer, reconciliation, and unity embraces all races and denominations.

And then Edwin Cole brings us to the issue of our word and God's Word. In this excerpt from *Strong Men in Tough Times* (Creation House, 1993), we see that our word is our bond, and that God's Word is His bond. Dr. Cole is founder and president of the Christian Men's Network. He is also a speaker, best-selling author, and motivational lecturer.

Setting a Sure Foundation

by
Jack Hayford

A teary-eyed blonde and crumbled buildings.

They seemed to have no relationship, but I couldn't escape the parallels they represented.

The first was a young woman, a sweet and lovely wife who had come to my office for counsel that morning. The second was the news report regarding thousands who were instantly crushed as buildings toppled from an earthquake in Mexico. The weeping wife poured out her heart that morning in my office. As she talked, I thought of the images I'd seen on television of mourning multitudes digging through rubble. The two disasters had the same root cause—negligence in building standards. Lousy foundations make for temporary homes.

The woman wasn't whiny or complaining. In fact, she hadn't volunteered any information that would pin the fault on her husband. I appreciated that: She was entirely ready to accept full responsibility for her situation. But the more I inquired, the clearer it became that whatever her shortcomings, there was a sad, underlying reason for the lack of development in her marriage. The man of the house *believed* in God but had no pattern whatsoever for *worshiping* Him.

Oh, the husband had some half-baked notions he would conveniently throw up like a "Hail Mary" football pass when faced with a desperate, need-an-

answer situation. You know what I mean; it goes like this: "I believe in worshiping God according to the dictates of my own conscience. I don't think you need to be in a church—I simply worship God from my heart, wherever I am. I think you can worship God as much in the mountains as in town at church. I want to be honest and sincere about worship, and I don't think people who try to prove their superiority over others by going to church are any better than me."

And the drone goes on. It's an empty argument concocted by a mind that has rarely, if ever, taken time to assess the shallowness of its foundational thought. Whatever may be correct in the "straw man" propositions, the basic goal isn't to assure sincere worship but to avoid commitment.

The Foundational Commitment

Who, how, and when a man worships determines everything about his life. That's the reason the first promise a man needs to keep is that *he'll be honest with God*. And honesty with the almighty God—the Creator of all things, including us; the Giver of all life, including ours; the Savior of all sinners, including us; and the Master of human destiny, including ours—*this* God—above and beyond all pretenders to His throne—demands attention to *His* ways of worship. The whimsy and flimsy of human reason, the puff and pride of human arrogance, only need to pass once through the flame of His presence to be shown for what they are: *Nothing*. And a life built with nothing at its center results in homes and relationships with nothing underneath them. Like the frustrated wife in my office, like the pancaked houses in Mexico, groundless "faith" and lack of commitment to worship result in homes without foundations and relationships without roots. When stress comes, they can't stand the test.

How can a man find the path to worship that pours substance into him, strength into his life's foundations, unshakable stability into his marriage, steadfastness into his relationships, and trustworthiness into his work and business practices? The answer is found by beginning where God has always started with men—at worship!

A Timeless Pattern

It's not as if the picture and principles aren't clear.

See God introducing Adam to *redeeming worship* in the garden, after sin had marred that setting and the promise of a Savior was given (see Gen. 3:15).

See God calling Abraham to *faith-filled worship* and promising to thereby make him an instrument of blessing to all the families of mankind (see Gen. 12:1-8).

See God calling Moses to *delivering worship*, showing how the sacrifice of the lamb would save enslaved households from death and open a future with meaning (see Exod. 12:1-28).

See God calling Isaiah to *purifying worship* as the young man stood in the presence of the Lord, stunned by God's greatness and humbled by his own sinfulness (see Isa. 6:1-5).

See the church born in *empowering worship* as God's Spirit began the era of our witness as believers in Jesus Christ—the church praising God and seeing supernatural grace bringing multitudes to Christ (see Acts 2).

Each of those expressions of worship has a counterpart in a man's life today. Each has an application that can forge solid "stuff" into the foundation of a Promise Keeper's life.

1. Redeeming Worship

Redeeming worship centers on the Lord's Table. Whether your tradition celebrates it as Communion, Eucharist, the Mass, or the Lord's Supper, we are all called to this centerpiece of Christian worship.

Jesus, the builder of the church, commanded that this regular practice be laid in the foundations of our observance as worshipers (see 1 Cor. 11:23-26). The power of the redeeming blood of Christ not only saves our souls, but it is also the foundation of all redemptive, recovering, renewing works of God.

2. Faith-filled Worship

Faith-filled worship calls for action. When Abraham heard God's voice, he broke with convenience, got up, and went where God said to go (see Gen. 12).

It isn't difficult to draw this analogy to one of the most fundamental calls you and I face every week: the wake-up call to gather with the people of God to worship Him. Listen to the call: "Let us not give up meeting together, as some are in the habit of doing, but let us encourage one another—and all the more as you see the Day approaching" (Heb. 10:25).

There's no escaping the fact that worship gets intensely practical at this point. It takes place (1) at a certain time, (2) at a certain place, (3) with a certain group, and (4) for very certain reasons. Try and spiritualize it anyway we please—or try to scorn "church" as traditional, ritualistic, passé, or boring—still the Bible lays down a mandate: Don't forsake it!

Yes, it costs inconvenience of schedule, preparation, tolerance, and grace, plus the humbling of ourselves. We need to get up, get going, get there on time, get a right attitude, get with the program, and get ready to receive from the input of others (who sometimes don't fascinate us all that much). The fruit of this commitment is the laying of strong foundations of practical faith—the *real* faith that follows God and affects others around us, as Abraham's did.

3. Delivering Worship

Delivering worship is that which frees a man from bondage, liberates his family to its greatest possibilities, and opens the way to the future without the entanglements of the past. That's what happened when Moses submitted to worship.

This type of worship was revealed most dramatically in two events that occurred within days of one another: the Passover in Egypt and Israel's passage through the Red Sea. The story that unfolds in the first 15 chapters of Exodus hinged on a private encounter between Moses and God Himself. What resulted was a man's household being set free and his own life finding its intended destiny. Walk through it with him.

1. *God calls a man into His fiery presence* (see Exod. 3:1-4). We should put away idle notions that worship can be tamed to our own tastes. The man who fears drawing near to the flame of God's Spirit at work will never experience a complete burning away of fear and pride.
2. *God calls a man to remove his shoes* (see Exod. 3:5). The issue wasn't bare feet but the removal of one's own self-fashioned support. In other words, God wanted of Moses and desires of us a will to put nothing of our own creation between ourselves and Him. And standing barefoot in the rocky terrain of a desert, as Moses did, will cause a man to walk more cautiously before God.
3. *God calls a man to know His heart* (see Exod. 3:7-8). Notice how it was in God's presence that Moses learned of God's gentle heart, loving concern, compassionate nature, and desire to heal and deliver. You and I need to be in His presence for the same reason. My family—yours, too—needs a husband and dad who is regularly being imbued with God's love, understanding, and gentleness.
4. *God calls a man to leadership* (see Exod. 3:9-10). For Moses, the call was to lead a nation, whereas your call and mine will likely

> be less visible. But make no mistake, we *are* leaders! And there is no avoiding the fact that people around us will be affected by whether or not we accept our call to God's purpose in our lives.

The bottom line of this whole encounter is *how* God showed Moses the way His purposes would be fulfilled in him. We read it in Exodus 3:11-12: "But Moses said to God, 'Who am I, that I should go to Pharaoh and bring the Israelites out of Egypt?' And God said, 'I will be with you. And this will be the sign to you that it is I who have sent you: When you have brought the people out of Egypt, you will worship God on this mountain.' "

Moses' response was as incredulous as yours or mine would be: "Who am I?" In short, the man was saying, "Hey, God, I know *You're* mighty, but I don't think I could ever become what You're saying I'm to become." God's answer was terse and direct: "You shall worship God on this mountain!" It was stated so briefly as to pass notice and put so simply as to defy belief. God was saying, "The answer to your question 'Who am I?' is in your *worshiping Me*. You will find who you are when you know who I am!"

Chuck was a hard-nosed guy, a tough, hard-hat type to whom worship seemed more suited for women and children. Sam was a business executive—in many ways the precise opposite of Chuck except for his conclusions about worship. They exemplified what I've found to be the most common presumptions by men who think worship too mystical, too holy, too "beyond" for them.

Both Chuck and Sam became part of our monthly men's gatherings where I had prioritized three things: (1) forthright, no-games-played *worship*, (2) honest, say-it-out-to-someone sharing in *prayer*, and (3) straight-from-the-shoulder, Bible-centered, practical *teaching*. I watched them, just as I've watched hundreds of others, break free through delivering worship. *Guys* who break the sound barrier and sing from the heart (no matter how bad their voices); *guys* who kneel humbly with a group of men, lifting their voices in concerted prayer; *guys* who express their surrender to the Almighty as Paul called men to do with upraised hands (see 1 Tim. 2:8)—*these guys change!*

4. Purifying Worship

Purifying worship comes from a man's *waiting* in the presence of God. Whatever may be said for the essential place of *corporate* worship in the church, there is still no substitute for *private* worship—meeting God alone.

Isaiah's record of his face-to-face meeting with the living God relates how ashamed he became of his impurity: " 'Woe to me!' I cried. 'I am ruined! For

I am a man of unclean lips, and I live among a people of unclean lips' " (Isa. 6:5). In short, "God, I'm stained, and I work in an atmosphere cluttered with foul mouths and ungodliness." Sound familiar?

However, I've met thousands of men who have surmounted the power of personal and societal uncleanness, of profanity, of mental impurity or foul habits. And they didn't accomplish it by the grit of self-imposed efforts at stringent discipline. They found purity through the power of being in God's presence!

Listen to Jesus' words: "Blessed are the pure in heart, for they will see God" (Matt. 5:8). Check this closely, because too many read this text to mean, "Everybody who's perfect will arrive in heaven some day." But Jesus wasn't talking about purity in ritual terms. He was talking about the fundamental definition: *Purity* is "that which is undiluted by other substances." Now, join that to the place Jesus pointed at, to the *heart* of a man—*that's* where God seeks undiluted commitment.

So what does it all mean? The answer is in what Jesus did and didn't say. He *didn't* say, "Blessed are the pure in mouth . . . hands . . . mind . . . feet." No. Christ calls you and me to come, candidly and with a *heart fully opened* in worship, into the privacy of His presence. Then something will happen: If we bring our whole heart, without restriction or reservation, we will see God!

That, my brother, doesn't mean you or I will have a phantasmic vision of heaven or see fleecy clouds with angels flying. It means we will become candidates for seeing God's *nature* take over our lives, God's *hand* provide for our needs, and God's *grace* work through our touch, words, and witness. *We will see God.* It's the privilege of the purified, not earned by accomplished holiness but realized through the total devotion of a man's heart at worship.

5. Empowering Worship

Empowering worship emerges from that quest for God that receptively opens to the fullness of His Holy Spirit. Acts 2 is a case study of men who had *walked* with Christ coming to the moment when they were *filled* with His Spirit and power. It happened in an atmosphere of worship.

The record of Scripture is expanded by the record of history; men who worship become men of spiritual power. It isn't because they have a mystical experience but because they are filled with the mightiness of Jesus. Their power isn't in self-gratifying displays of personal accomplishment but in humble service, faith-filled prayer, and their availability to allow the Holy

Spirit to deliver His gifts through their lives.

Worship also sustains this divine empowering. Being filled doesn't guarantee being full today. That's why the apostle Paul commanded, "Keep on being filled with the Holy Spirit" (Eph. 5:18, my literal translation). Then he prescribed the way to such sustained fullness: "Speak to one another with psalms, hymns and spiritual songs. Sing and make music in your heart to the Lord" (Eph. 5:19). There it is, put as clearly as possible: *Worship sustains Holy Spirit fullness*. A life of power is maintained by a man's daily spending time in God's presence—praising Him.

Present Yourself to God

No text in the Bible makes it more clear:

> Therefore, I urge you, brothers, in view of God's mercy, to offer your bodies as living sacrifices, holy and pleasing to God—this is your spiritual act of worship. Do not conform any longer to the pattern of this world, but be transformed by the renewing of your mind. Then you will be able to test and approve what God's will is—his good, pleasing and perfect will. (Rom. 12:1-2)

Those pointed words call for a man's entire being—body, mind, emotions, spirit—to be presented to God in worship. The result is *transformation* from world-mindedness to Christ-mindedness, and *proof* of the will of God—which is demonstrated and verified in his life.

The infusion of this kind of "stuff" into a man puts substance in his character, concrete in his family's foundation, holy steel in his soul's strength, and weight in his person and presence. The Promise Keeper's first priority is *worship*. For in meeting the Almighty, the foundation for all of life's "promises yet to keep" is laid in the unshakableness of His being. It's the strongest place any of us can stand.

And we stand best when we've first learned to kneel: *worshiping*.

Why Men Must Pray

by
Wellington Boone

Today, we are faced with cultures around the world in steady decline. The number of violent crimes in the United States, for example, has increased 570 percent since 1960, while the population increased only 43 percent. Over the same period, illegitimate births increased more than 400 percent. The U.S. has the highest rates of teen pregnancy, abortion, and childbirth in the industrialized world. From 1960 to 1993, Scholastic Aptitude Test scores dropped 67 points. I could go on and on, but you get the picture. There's no doubt that the situation is grim. What can we men possibly do to make a difference?

Well, for one thing, we can pray for revival.

Before you dismiss that idea as simplistic, consider that this isn't the first time a country has faced such a crisis. In 1735, Wales was in decline politically and spiritually. There was an upsurge of the occult and the renewed practice of divination and black magic.

In that same year, a young man named Howell Harris was converted to Christianity. Soon after, Harris was praying in the village where he was a teacher, and God met him in a powerful way. Nothing seemed impossible to him. He began to travel everywhere, preaching, until all of South Wales was awakened. Even notorious criminals were converted and changed their ways.

The secret of Harris's influence on the masses was prayer. He understood that nothing would be accomplished, either in himself or in his troubled nation, without prayer—personal, private communion with God.

In every generation, revival has come as the result of prayer. For example, powerful prayer preceded America's First Great Awakening, which gave the colonists a unified biblical view of the principles of freedom and helped pave the way for the American Revolution. The Second Great Awakening, which preceded America's Civil War, brought a conviction from God that slavery was a sin. It was led by men like Charles Finney, who prayed for hours upon hours and days upon days.

God still needs men who, like Howell Harris and Charles Finney, will give themselves to prayer and then go and do whatever the Holy Spirit tells them.

Revival is the movement of the Holy Spirit in an extraordinary way that causes multitudes to be drawn to Christ. That's what we need today. Our world needs revival. The church needs revival. Families need revival. Men need revival.

The prayer that sparks revival begins long before the countryside seems to awaken from its slumber in sin. It starts when men fall on their knees and cry out to God. That's where true intimacy with God takes place and we begin the journey of being transformed into the image of Christ. And as men are transformed, the course of a nation can be changed.

The need for revival to start within the praying individual was brought home to me powerfully a few years ago. I was driving across the United States from my home in Virginia on what I call a prayer sabbatical, something I do every year to get alone with God. As I drove along, praying, I asked God to change hearts in the inner city and bring another great awakening. Suddenly, the biblical story of blind Bartimaeus flashed through my mind. He hated being blind, and I was stirred by his zeal. When he heard Jesus approaching, he cried out, "Jesus, Son of David, have mercy on me!" (Mark 10:47).

Then I thought, *I'm blind, too, because I don't know my own heart. I'm praying God would move on the inner cities, but I need Him to move on me. Bartimaeus had more desire for the healing of his physical blindness than I have for the healing of my spiritual blindness.*

At that realization, I cried out loud in the car, "Jesus, Son of David, have mercy on me!" Who was I to pray for change in others when I myself remained unchanged? That experience began a revival in me that still today influences my life and ministry.

We need to see our own hearts so God can change us—personal revival—

and then use us to improve our homes, our workplaces, our churches, and all of society.

Before I suggest some steps in the process of life-changing prayer, let me warn that one of the greatest hindrances to developing a personal relationship with God is packaged programs that tell you how to pray. A man must be drawn to God alone, there to find his own "how-to's."

Moses found God in the burning bush.

David wrote many of his prayers in the form of poetry and music.

Elijah hid in a cave and heard God's still, small voice.

Jesus met with the Father in the wilderness.

You need to find for yourself the things that keep your prayer relationship with God fresh. However, most people can benefit from a few practical suggestions to help them understand where to begin.

The Holy Spirit leads us into a personal prayer relationship with God through four stages. I believe they are inevitable steps in the growing process where we move from focusing on our own needs to focusing on the privilege of worshiping God. After all, worship, in its truest sense, means giving ourselves to God. It means forgetting about ourselves for the sheer joy of knowing Him.

These four words summarize the four stages of entering into a prayer relationship with God: love, intimacy, privilege, and responsibility. Let's look at each of them in turn.

Love

The initiative of love is always first with the Father. "For God so loved the world that he gave his one and only Son, that whoever believes in him shall not perish but have eternal life" (John 3:16). Even our salvation is a response to God's love. Scripture says it is the goodness of God that leads men to repentance.

The first time we yield to God is when we come to Him for salvation. We acknowledge our sinfulness. We thank Him for giving His Son to be our Savior. He embraces us. We are immersed in His love. And we find oneness with the Father.

Intimacy

When we're alone with God, there are no more distractions to the development of intimacy. It is just us and Him. The rest of the world must wait.

True prayer is not a rhetorical stream of eloquent words. It is the expression of a deep longing for God that is born out of love. When we're in love with someone, we always look for ways to spend time with the person. We press through with the development of the relationship in every way.

Finding God is the beginning. Getting to know Him is the journey. Scores of people have found Him in saving grace but have not yet come to know Him in intimacy, the place where He begins to impart a sense of divine separation for His purposes.

Privilege

Out of the atmosphere of intimacy, trust is born. Where there is trust, there is the granting of privilege. What a privilege to understand and know God! What a privilege to comprehend Him through a living relationship! The greatest privilege any believer can have is access before almighty God with the confidence that He will answer prayer.

Responsibility

If we truly believe Christ is alive, we will do anything for Him because we can believe God for anything and we know He is omnipresent. We know He identifies with us as His body. We recognize He is not only Lord over our lives, but He also takes responsibility for us and gives us responsibilities to carry out for Him.

When God grants you the privilege of knowing Him, He does not do it so you can get your needs met. He does it so He can accomplish His will. Unanswered prayer is a failure to approach God on the basis of His will, because "this is the confidence we have in approaching God: that if we ask anything *according to his will*, he hears us" (1 John 5:14, emphasis added).

Praying for Revival

One thing we know God wants His people to pray for is revival. But if revival is to come, there must be a change in the prayer lives of men worldwide. It is time for us to return to our knees and remain there until something happens.

The prophet Hosea said, "Sow for yourselves righteousness, reap the fruit of unfailing love, and break up your unplowed ground; for it is time to seek the LORD, until he comes and showers righteousness on you" (Hosea 10:12). God is looking for a company of men of courage who are willing to do whatever it takes to bring another great spiritual awakening.

In our ministry, we have an acronym for the type of prayer life that is necessary to bring about change. The word is ***P.U.S.H.*,** which stands for:

Pray Until Something Happens.

That acronym also stands for four steps you need to take in order to see personal, family, and national revival.

***P*: Purify yourself.**

Search your heart. Repent from any known sin. The prophet Hosea said, "Sow for yourselves righteousness." Paul wrote, "Let us purify ourselves from everything that contaminates body and spirit, perfecting holiness out of reverence for God" (2 Cor. 7:1).

You need to sow the Word of God into yourself until you see that you are a sinner under the searchlight of God's righteousness. The psalmist wrote, "The unfolding of your words gives light" (Psa. 119:130). When you sin, be quick to turn away from it and cry out for God's mercy.

***U*: Understand God's mercy.**

We need to receive mercy from God, and we need to deliver mercy as ambassadors for Christ to a lost generation. "Be merciful to those who doubt" (Jude 22). Jesus said, "Blessed are the merciful, for they will be shown mercy" (Matt. 5:7).

Your personal revival awaits your willingness to forgive all who have wronged you and to seek forgiveness of others you have wronged (see Mark 11: 25-26).

***S*: Sanctify yourself.**

Learn to live a life of personal accountability to God. Regardless of what others consider to be righteous, keep yourself "from being polluted by the world" (James 1:27). Be separated for the purposes of God. "As God has said, I will live with them and walk among them, and I will be their God, and they will be my people. Therefore come out from them and be separate, says the Lord" (2 Cor. 6:16-17).

Separation for God does not mean we leave the world or neglect our families. Just the opposite. It means that our commitment to the living, righteous, holy God becomes evident to all those around us.

Hosea said, "Break up your unplowed ground." We must learn to immediately obey everything God tells us to do. We never want to have a wrong heart toward Him.

H: Hold fast in prayer.

Pray Until Something Happens. Prayer is work. It is blessed work, but it *is* work. As in any relationship, it takes effort to give up some of your own pleasures to bring pleasure to another. The chief sin of the church today is laziness. We are lazy about prayer. We're lazy about changing ourselves. We're lazy about good works. We're certainly lazy about praying through for a great spiritual awakening in our contry.

God has made available incredible power to change this nation, and yet we remain in our dulled state of sin, complaining about the condition of our nation, crime in the inner cities, and corruption among politicians.

Just think of all the power that could be unleashed if the 50,000 men who attended the Promise Keepers rally in Colorado in 1993 would begin to P.U.S.H. for America. What would happen if each of those men made a commitment to Pray Until Something Happens? Can you see what a serious force that would be? What if that same commitment happened in other countries of the world?

The Power for Revival

Our problem is that we have no understanding of the great power within us. We're unwilling to give up our comforts, like morning sleep, for a few precious moments with God. "I love them that love me; and those that seek me early shall find me" (Prov. 8:17, KJV).

We call ourselves men of God, but we are too often men of our own needs. All needs are met on our knees. We must substitute "knees" for "needs."

America, for example, is sick and dying because the people have lost hope and vision (see Prov. 29:18). Even the church is aimless. Why? Primarily because of a lack of faith in God. But why do people lack faith? Because those who say they are men of God are so seemingly helpless to bring about change. They say they pray and study the Word, but their wives and children see little evidence in their lives. Our prayer and study lives should have an immediate, ongoing effect on our families. They should be so moved by our love and mercy that they want to emulate what they see in us of the character and qualities of Christ.

Do we really believe that Jesus has risen from the dead and that God answers prayer? If we do—if we continually develop that perspective through time with God on our knees—we will become the source of faith, hope, and vision that the world so desperately needs.

When the world sees men of God overcome with the lusts and pride of the self-life and trying to find a sense of purpose, however, its vision of God is distorted. A passage in Isaiah captures well the futility of our nation's Christian men over the past 30 or so years: "As a woman with child and about to give birth. . . . We were with child, we writhed in pain, but we gave birth to wind. We have not brought salvation to the earth" (Isa. 26:17-18).

The Next Great Awakening

But by God's grace, on our knees, that is all changing. Promise Keepers have become impregnated with personal revival. Our changed lives are obvious. Like a woman who is pregnant and nearing the end of her term, we Christian men are about to burst forth with the coming of the Lord in ways we have never experienced.

"In the last days, God says, I will pour out my Spirit on all people" (Acts 2:17). We have not had our last revival.

" 'Before she goes into labor, she gives birth; before the pains come upon her, she delivers a son. Who has ever heard of such a thing? Who has ever seen such things? Can a country be born in a day or a nation be brought forth in a moment? Yet no sooner is Zion in labor than she gives birth to her children. Do I bring to the moment of birth and not give delivery?' says the Lord. 'Do I close up the womb when I bring to delivery?' says your God" (Isa. 66:7-9).

I believe that the church is in travail and that God is about to birth the next great awakening. And it will start with Promise Keepers on their knees in prayer.

Your Word Is Your Bond

by
Edwin Louis Cole

The men in the outdoor stadium numbered 22,000. They cheered, clapped, shouted, and slapped each other on the back with wild enthusiasm. They laughed, cried, and even sang together like no sports, military, or political crowd I'd ever seen. This was not a riot, sporting event, or review of some country's fighting men. It was a gathering of Christians, and the occasion was a celebration of their manhood under the lordship of Jesus Christ.

As I prepared to address them, I shivered a little. Would my words be adequate? How could I sum up 13 years of teaching in one short hour? What single major theme did the Lord want to get across above any others? I had settled on the subject Coach Bill McCartney had heard me teach years before.

Looking out over that football stadium on a midsummer's day, I started the men off as I do in most of my men's meetings, slapping "high-fives" and forcefully greeting others with, "Thank God you're a man!" As I watched them smiling, pumping hands, and sharing the joy of being men, I could not help but swell with admiration for Coach McCartney and his courage and faith in calling for such an event. He was living out his goal to awaken men to the need of being men of their word.

My part in Promise Keepers that year was the Saturday morning meeting. The men were enthusiastic and excited, ready for the day. My heart pounded as they took their seats and I gave them the words I felt God had inspired me to say. And just as I presented the message that day, I lay it out for you here.

A major sign of manhood is in a man's word. To be conformed to the image of Christ (see Rom. 8:29), our words must conform to God's Word. God's Word is tough; it outlasts tough times.

Five Propositions Concerning God's Word

Here are five vital truths concerning God's Word:

1. God's Word is His bond.

When God made a promise to Abraham, because He could swear by nothing greater, He swore by Himself (see Heb. 6:13). In the new covenant established long after Abraham, in which Jesus Christ is the mediator, Jesus Himself is the Word that confirms the promise of salvation.

2. God's Word is the expression of His nature.

Jesus came to earth as the "express image" of the person of God (see Heb. 1:3). He told Philip, "Anyone who has seen me has seen the Father" (John 14:9, TLB).

John 1:1 states, "In the beginning was the Word, and the Word was with God, and the Word was God." As the rest of John 1 makes clear, Jesus is that living Word of God. Because God's Word is the expression of His nature, when Christ came, it was necessary He be the Word made flesh (see John 1:14). The very nature of God is revealed in Him. Likewise, Jesus is revealed in the written Word. As Jesus is God's Word revealed, so the Bible is God's Word revealed to us. And the Word is made alive in our hearts by the Holy Spirit.

3. God's Word is the measure of His character.

When Jesus referred to Himself as the Alpha and Omega, He was using the first and last letters of the Greek alphabet (see Rev. 1:8). In other words, He is the beginning and the end. If He were using the English alphabet, He would say, "I am the A and Z."

Think how many times the 26 letters in the English alphabet have been used, in words spoken and written, since its inception. Yet it is still as new as the day it was invented. The words may have changed in meaning, spelling, or writing, but the alphabet itself—its capacity to form new words and express new meanings—is undiminished, interminable, and immeasurable. So, too, is Jesus.

Think of all the sermons that have been preached from the Word of God; all the revelation from the Word that is known; the books written concerning it; how much it's being used today—yet it's still as new as the day it was given. There is no end to God's character, and thus no end to His Word. No matter how much of Himself He reveals, even in eternity, there will be no end to the revelation of His character. The measure of God's character is in His Word.

4. God's Word is magnified above His name.

God's name is as good as His Word. If His Word were no good, His name would be no good.

Faith comes by hearing, and hearing by the Word of God, the Bible says (see Rom. 10:17). The prayer of faith is always made on the basis of His Word. The use of His name is predicated on His Word. When Jesus said to use His name (see Mark 16:17), He was literally telling us to use His authority.

5. God's Word is the sole source of faith and the absolute rule of conduct.

"There is no other name under heaven given to men by which we must be saved"—only the name of Jesus Christ (Acts 4:12). God's Word alone—Jesus—accepted by faith, has the power of salvation. And once saved, "Man does not live on bread alone, but on every word that comes from the mouth of God" (Matt. 4:4). God's Word stands sure.

The Importance of Our Word

History has a way of repeating itself, and though culture may change, the nature of man remains the same. We live in a day not unlike that of the prophet Isaiah. At one time, he told his generation and nation that their transgressions were not unknown to them (see Isa. 59:12). The sins that testified against them were in "rebellion and treachery against the LORD, turning our backs on our God, fomenting oppression and revolt, uttering lies our hearts have conceived" (Isa. 59:13). Isaiah said that "justice is driven back, and righteousness stands at a distance" (Isa. 59:14).

Men familiar with the standard of God's Word know the sins of their countries, how people have mistreated one another and rebelled against constituted authority in cities and homes. For me in the United States, it seems at times that judgment is turned backward and our system of jurisprudence is more concerned about the rights of criminals than those of victims. Justice seems to be "driven back" in that it's hard for the common man to find, yet it appears that certain people can buy it.

Isaiah, speaking by the Spirit of God, said the reason for our ills is that truth "has stumbled in the streets. . . . [It is] nowhere to be found" (Isa. 59:14-15).

Recently, as I prepared for my first ministry trip to a part of the world newly liberated from communism, I talked with a gentleman from that nation. "I feel impressed," I told him, "that I should speak on God's Word and man's word and how important it is to be men of our word and lovers of truth."

"In my country," he said slowly, with a kind but sad expression, "you will first have to teach us what truth is. My people no longer know."

In the aftermath of the collapse of communism, people of his nation came to the terrible realization that their leaders had been lying to them for years. In the trauma of learning of the lies and trying to find the truth, many citizens openly preferred to go back to the way things were. At least then they could believe something in ignorance. Discovering truth was as hard for them as digging for gold and silver. They didn't know what to believe, and rather than trying to find the truth, they were content with a lie.

A recent *Time* magazine cover article titled "Lying" featured the epidemic plague in the national character of the U.S. The writer advanced a premise that "everyone does it." Because of its prevalence, lying was viewed as the norm rather than the exception. But as a letter to the editor later scolded, "I can think of no better way to encourage lying than to tell people that 'everyone's doing it'!" (*Time*, Oct. 26, 1992, p. 6).

The propositions of God's Word and the overwhelming absence of truth in the world today have tremendous relevance to the way men live. The book of Genesis recounts the creation of man and states that Adam was created in the image of God, including His moral likeness (see Gen. 1:26-27). God invested Himself in Adam. In that divine bestowment, God endowed man with creative power, in his loins and in his mouth.

That humanity is able to reproduce in the image of God is one of the greatest wonders of the universe. What is formed in the womb is a creation like unto Almighty God. To make the womb the tomb, to destroy what God ordained to be in His image, is sacrilege done to God Himself.

Creative power is also in a man's word. Man speaks into existence things and ideas that have never been before. Incredibly, Scripture says the tongue has the power of life and death (see Prov. 18:21). Therefore, words must be spoken in the fear of the Lord, and we will have to account for every idle word (see Matt. 12:36).

Five Propositions Concerning Our Word

Because we're created in the image of God, whatever God's Word is to Him, our word is to be to us. God watches over His Word to perform it. So should we. The same truths relative to God's Word apply to ours.

1. Our word is our bond.

I remember from my youth when men's character was much stronger and richer in integrity. The moral climate was such that lying, cheating, and stealing were gross sins. Those caught in them were dismissed from school, barred from practicing law, voted out of public office, and ruined in reputation. When a man gave you his word and shook your hand, it was better than a signed contract; it was a covenant. Often no written contract was necessary—a man's word was his bond.

Such is not the rule today. Lawyers draw up legal papers with infinite pains to cover every detail of the agreement. Yet the paper is only as good as the character of the people who sign it. Even in marriage, men still vow to remain wed "until death do us part," but too often they treat their vow as part of a ritual without true meaning. In many cases, that phrase has even been eliminated from the marriage vows. I heard one pastor say, "Why make them lie at their wedding?"

When men don't hold to a high value of truth, they don't place a high value on their word, either.

2. Our word is the expression of our nature.

In the early days of my Christian experience, we were taught to "sanctify our speech," because a person's words reveal the nature within. *Gosh* and *darn* were considered euphemisms for *God* and *damn*. Such minced oaths were consciously removed from our vocabularies. So concerned were we with our word that we regularly practiced using King James English. When Nancy and I traveled with our children through Nevada, we joked that we wouldn't even say "Hoover Dam" but instead "Hoover Water-stopper."

Salvation was, to us, a total experience. Inside and out, the Holy Spirit was at work to cleanse us from all unrighteousness.

The world uses the name of Christ profanely in its swearing, while Christians swear by His name. A man who uses the name of Jesus as an epithet in everyday conversation cannot be truthful on Sunday in worshiping that name. The idea of purging our language may need to be revived.

3. Our word is the measure of our character.

The honesty of a man's heart, the depth of his character, is shown by how he keeps his word. It's called *integrity*. Job cried out in his deepest need, "I will not deny my integrity" (Job 27:5).

God commended Job to Satan by saying, "He still maintains his integrity" (Job 2:3).

Job's wife, in exasperation after all his possessions were gone, cried out against him, "Are you still holding on to your integrity? Curse God and die!" (Job 2:9). But he would not.

Men who prove their integrity are held in admiration and great respect. As Scripture says, a man with integrity is one who "keeps his oath even when it hurts" (Psa. 15:4). In other words, he keeps his word even if it costs him.

4. Our word is magnified above our name.

Our name is only as good as our word. If our word is no good, neither is our name.

Men who don't value their word diminish their personal worth. An amazing number of people submit false resumés for professional positions. Men exaggerate and women lie; then when they're discovered, they fight because they're fired. But regardless of the quality of their work, their value drops sharply when they are deemed untrustworthy.

5. Our word is the source of faith and rule of conduct for those to whom we give it.

God is a maximizer of men; Satan is a usurper. Christ is truth; Satan is the father of lies (see John 8:44). Satan has the character of a thief who steals, kills, and destroys (see John 10:10). Satan attacks God's Word to lure men into sin. And if he attacks God's Word, it's obvious he will also attack man's word to lure into sin the man and those who trust him.

When Satan approached Eve in the Garden of Eden, his accusation against God's Word undermined her faith. Adam eventually denied God's right of possession, rejected His sovereignty, and was expelled from His presence. By attacking God's Word, Satan stole Adam and Eve's faith, killed their relationship with God, and destroyed their lives. His attacks on men's lives today likewise start with God's Word. Satan's subtle scheme is to attack God's Word and promise us "true" liberty while putting us in bondage. *All sin promises to serve and please but only desires to enslave and dominate.*

In His parable of the sower and the seed, Jesus told us that immediately after the Word is sown, Satan comes to steal it (see Mark 4:13-20). Immediately after conversion comes the temptation to deny the reality of the experience. People discount it, relatives mock it, and the desire for old habits increases. If we don't stay close to the Lord, God's Word can be stolen, our faith can be killed, and our relationship with God can be ruined. But overcoming the attack on God's Word by reading and speaking it concentrates and confirms our relationship with Him.

Satan not only tries to "rip off" God's Word, but he tries to steal our word as well. Think of a father who promises to take his son fishing. The son immediately prepares, putting the tackle box and fishing pole under his bed while he dreams of the day. Then the night before their fishing trip, the father's friend calls with tickets to a football game, and the father accepts his offer.

Early the next morning, the son is up, eager to get going, only to be told his dad is going to the game instead. Disappointed, the son sulks and later refuses to come to dinner until threatened. Days of resentful attitude follow until, in exasperation, the father tells the son to change or be punished. The boy's disappointment turns to resentment, then deepens into rebellion. Without realizing his own culpability, the father repeats his behavior and helplessly watches the hardening of his son's heart.

What about the man who constantly promises his wife that he will change but always reneges, or that he will give her things or take her places but never does? Little does he realize he is teaching her not to trust his word. *Trust is extended to the limit of truth and no more.*

Tough? Yeah, that's tough. But real? You bet!

I've listened to men who even give God their word and then fail to keep it. They don't realize their word is being ripped off. Their enemy is their own shallow character that doesn't have enough strength in it, and also the satanic conspiracy to steal their words, kill their influence, and destroy their success and relationships.

No wonder God is calling men across the width and breadth of the earth to repent (see Acts 17:30)! It is time for every man to put away lying and to "speak truthfully" with God and his neighbor (Eph. 4:25). Reverence for God's Word means reverence for *your* word. You were created in the image of God. Be a man of God's Word. Be a man of your own word!

Remember . . .

- God's Word is His bond.
- As God's Word is to Him, our word is to be to us.
- Your name is only as good as your word.

- Your word is the source of faith and rule of conduct for those to whom you give it.
- All sin promises to serve and please but only desires to enslave and dominate.
- Trust is extended to the limit of truth and no more.

(Adapted from *Strong Men in Tough Times*, by Edwin Louis Cole, © copyright 1993. Used by permission of Creation House, Altamonte Springs, Florida.)

A Man and His God
Personal Evaluation

On a scale from 1 to 10, rate yourself in the following areas, with 1 being very weak and 10 being perfect.

1. I have committed my life totally to Jesus Christ. _____
2. I am involved in worshiping God according to the biblical pattern. ____
3. I am committed to Pray Until Something Happens. _____
4. My word is my bond. _____
5. God's Word is my source of faith and rule of conduct._____

Now review the list. Of the five areas listed above, which one requires your attention first?

In the Group

1. Describe in 60 seconds or less what worship was like in your home as a boy. (Each member should do this.)
2. In 60 seconds, tell about a time you prayed and how (or if) your prayer was answered. (Each member should do this.)
3. Has anything happened this past week to validate or demonstrate your commitment to Jesus Christ?
4. How can you begin your day by honoring Jesus?
5. Whose word do you trust more than any other person's? What can you do this week to help others believe your word?
6. What one thing would you like the men in your group to pray about? (Each member should do this.) Close your time with prayer together. Each man can say a one-sentence prayer for the person on his right, according to the need that man expressed.

Memory Verse: "Therefore, I urge you, brothers, in view of God's mercy, to offer your bodies as living sacrifices, holy and pleasing to God—this is your spiritual act of worship. Do not conform any longer to the pattern of this world, but be transformed by the renewing of your mind. Then you will be able to test and approve what God's will is—his good, pleasing and perfect will" (Rom. 12:1-2).

On Your Own

1. Write a prayer to start your day. Make it 30 words or less in length. Use it to begin each day this coming week.
2. Read the next section, "A Man and His Mentors," before the next meeting.

Promise 2

A Man and His Mentors

A Promise Keeper is committed to pursuing vital relationships with a few other men, understanding that he needs brothers to help him keep his promises.

PROMISE 2

Introduction

Such a big commitment as we have made in Promise 1—to honor Jesus Christ through worship, prayer, and obedience to His Word—cannot be fulfilled alone. We need like-minded friends. We need support, encouragement, and maybe even an occasional boot in the rear to help us keep that and the other commitments called for in this book.

God never intended for us to do it alone. No doubt, there are men around you who are way down the road of maturity in their faith. Likewise, there are others who have just started the journey and could use the help of a friend like you. The concept of those who are more mature helping those who are less mature is called *mentoring*. Some Christian traditions speak of spiritual directors, shepherds, or even spiritual fathers. Regardless of the name you give them, we all need mentors.

Dr. Howard Hendricks and Dr. E. Glenn Wagner are well equipped to guide us in this area. Dr. Hendricks is a distinguished professor at Dallas Theological Seminary, and thousands of his former students, active in ministry around the world, affectionately call him "Prof." Mentoring is the heart of his more than four decades of teaching success. He will lay out for us the mandate for mentoring.

Dr. Wagner is Vice President of National Ministries for Promise Keepers. He will help us with the nitty-gritty of building relationships with other men. It's a sad fact that many men have no close friendships. Glenn will show us why that is and how to break through those barriers into meaningful friendship.

A Mandate for Mentoring

by
Dr. Howard G. Hendricks

The most compelling question every Christian man must ask is this: What am I doing today that will guarantee my impact for Jesus Christ in the next generation?

If I understand my New Testament correctly, there are only two things God is going to take off our planet. One is His Word, and the other is His people. If you are building His Word into people, you can be confident that will last forever.

That's why I am so passionate about mentoring. Mentoring is a ministry of multiplication. Every time you build into the life of another man, you launch a process that ideally will never end.

My life and ministry are the result of mentoring. I am a product of a core of individuals who built into my life ever since I came to Jesus Christ 60 years ago. One in particular, Walt, literally changed the course of my life.

I was born into a broken home in the city of Philadelphia. My parents were separated before I was born. I never saw them together except once—when I was called to testify in a divorce court. I'm sure I could have been reared, died, and gone to hell, and nobody would particularly have cared, except that a small group of believers got together in my neighborhood to start an evangelical church. That small group of individuals developed a passion for their community.

Walt belonged to that church, and he went to the Sunday school superintendent and said, "I want to teach a Sunday school class."

The superintendent said, "Wonderful, Walt, but we don't have any boys. Go out into the community. Anybody you pick up—that's your class."

I'll never forget the day I met him. Walt was six feet, four inches tall. He said to me as a little kid, "Hey, son, how would you like to go to Sunday school?"

Well, anything that had "school" in it had to be bad news.

Then he said, "How would you like to play marbles?"

That was different! Would you believe we got down and played marbles, and he beat me in every single game? I lost my marbles early in life! By the time Walt got through, I didn't care where he was going—that's where I wanted to go.

For your information, he picked up 13 of us boys, nine from broken homes. Today, 11 are in full-time vocational Christian work. And Walt never went to school beyond the sixth grade.

That's the power of a mentor. You don't need a Ph.D. to be used by God in the ministry of mentoring.

Have you ever asked, "Who has most affected my life?" Think about the people who made a difference. What did they do? How did they do it? Why did they do it? Answer those questions and you will be hooked on mentoring the rest of your life.

Why Mentoring?

I want to ask and answer two central questions, then apply those answers to your life. The first question is, *Why be concerned about mentoring?* Is this just another gimmick? Is this simply some secular idea imported from the corporate world that we've introduced into the Christian community and baptized with a few verses of Scripture? Or is it a biblically legitimate strategy for our generation?

I am convinced there are three compelling reasons you must become involved in a ministry of mentoring. First, *you need to be involved in mentoring because of the severe shortage of leaders*. Leaders are fast becoming an endangered species. Wherever I go, across America or around the world, the screaming need is for leaders. I meet few churches or Christian organizations that can afford to hang a sign outside their front door saying, "No Help Wanted."

We need leaders in our churches. The average church in America is operated by 15 to 20 percent of its membership. But God gives to *every* believer a spiritual gift with which to function in the body, not to spectate in the stands.

I tell my students there are only two groups of people in church: the pillars who support it and the caterpillars who crawl in and out week after week. The latter occupy 18 inches, more or less, on a pew, shake your hand as a pastor, and say with something of a pious whine, "Pastor, that was a wonderful message. We'll see you next week." They seldom come closer to the truth, for the fact is that 80 percent of the churches in America have plateaued or are in serious decline.

We need leaders in our homes, too. The American family is unraveling like a cheap sweater. May I remind you of one historical fact: No nation has ever survived the disintegration of its home life. Once the home goes, it's just a question of time before it all goes.

Pierre Mornell, distinguished West Coast psychiatrist, wrote a book titled *Passive Men, Wild Women*, and in that book he says,

> Over the last few years I've seen in my office an increasing number of couples who share a common denominator. The man is active, articulate, energetic, and usually successful in his work. But he is inactive, inarticulate, lethargic, and withdrawn at home. In his relationship with his wife he is passive. And his passivity drives her crazy. In the face of his retreat, she goes wild. (New York: Ballantine, 1979, p. 1)

Where are the men willing to step up to the plate and assume the leadership role God has given them in their homes?

We need leaders in our society as well. In politics, in business, in industry, in education, in agriculture, in the professions, in the military. I don't need to remind you that the landscape is littered with the bodies of men who have forfeited their right to be leaders because they were not men of integrity. They were not men we could trust.

Second, *we need mentoring because of the perceived need for mentors*. There's a severe deficiency in our culture, and it's seen in a number of areas. The first is the absence of fathers. I'm not talking only about physically absent; I'm talking about fathers who are emotionally and spiritually absent. The result is that the average boy in our society grows up and doesn't have a clue what a good father looks like.

The pedestals are empty! There's a shortage of older male models. It was well expressed by a little kid in a barbershop some time ago when I asked, "Hey, son, whom do you want to be like?"

He looked me straight in the eye and said, "Mister, I ain't found nobody I want to be like."

Do you think he's an exception? No, there is a terrifying void of affirming maleness in our society.

Recently my wife and I were in Jerusalem, visiting the Wailing Wall. We counted five bar mitzvahs going on. It was an exciting thing to watch those boys hoisted on the shoulders of their fathers, uncles, and friends, paraded around that sacred area with people clapping and singing, and women throwing candy. Those boys will never forget that day. But what do we have in American or other societies that even partially replicates that?

Someone asked me in a television interview, "What would you say has been your greatest contribution as a seminary professor?"

I answered, "To affirm the maleness of many of my students."

That's what we must do as men. Everywhere I go—to the university campus, evangelical churches, or the business and professional community—I find many young men asking, "Where can I find a mature friend?" And I find most older men asking, "Where can I find a ministry?" The result is the younger men are frustrated and the older men are unfulfilled. Intellectual honesty compels me to tell you: I find more younger men looking for older men to mentor them than I find older men willing to become involved in the lives of younger men. I say that to our shame.

Third, *we need mentoring because of the rape of existing leadership.* Two of the greatest curses ever perpetrated on a society have been crammed down our throats. One of them is the generation gap. There is no generation gap in the body of the Christ! You cannot drill any man out of the corps regardless of his age. Young people desperately need older people, and older people seriously need younger people who are going to carry on in the next generation.

The second curse is that of retirement. Retirement is a cultural, not a biblical, concept. You may retire from your company—you may not have an option—but you never retire from the Christian life and ministry. The only thing society knows to do with older men is to put them out to pasture and encourage them to play with the toys they have accumulated.

Have you noticed how many men there are over 50 who are reaching for the bench, who are sliding for home? At the very time when they ought to be tearing the place apart for Jesus Christ, they're caving in. May I remind you, the statistics are alarming of how many men die shortly after retirement. The reason is simple—they have no purpose for living. I'm finding an increasing number of guys blowing out their aorta on the way to Sarasota. The result? We're losing a great leadership pool in the body of Christ.

What Is Mentoring?

You say, "I'm convinced, but *what is mentoring?*" That's our second key question.

Let me answer with a simple definition. Mentoring is a process involving people.

Sometimes it's a whole series of individuals that God brings into your life at various stages and for various purposes. In every case, those people are committed to helping you grow and perpetuate the learning process.

The apostle Peter, in 2 Peter 3:18, said: "Grow in the grace and knowledge of our Lord and Savior Jesus Christ." He was saying, "As long as you live, you learn. And as long as you learn, you live."

Unfortunately, the epitaph of many a man is well expressed in the words "Died, age 26; buried, age 64."

If you stop learning and growing today, you stop ministering tomorrow.

Bear in mind that mentoring is not a new concept. The trades, the arts, and the guilds have engaged in mentoring for centuries. Craftsmen not only know what to do and how to do it, but they also know *why* they do *what* they're doing. They're suffused with basic attitudes, particularly a pride in their work. And they know what to get excited about!

All of us know about the great artist Michelangelo. But few know about Bertoldo, his teacher. There's a debate in art circles about who was the greater—Michelangelo, the pupil, or Bertoldo, the teacher who produced him.

Christian mentors are people who have a spiritual commitment. They're not playing games; they're committed to life change. And they have specific values. High on their priority list is the development in another individual of excellence so that the individual grows in his Christian life to hate the mania of mediocrity, the attitude that anything is good enough for God.

Not only is mentoring a person or a group of people, but it is also a process of developing a person to his maximum potential for Jesus Christ. In Colossians 1:28-29 we read, "We proclaim him, admonishing and teaching everyone with all wisdom." Why? "So that we may present everyone [mature] in Christ." And Paul added, "To this end I labor, struggling with all his energy, which so powerfully works in me."

Why was the apostle Paul committed to mentoring? Because he had clear-cut objectives. Your objectives determine your outcome. You achieve that for which you aim. Paul knew that the most important contribution he could make in terms of the next generation was to build into the life of the present one.

I'm finding an increasing number of men who are ending their lives at the top of the pile in terms of their field and at the bottom in terms of fulfillment. I believe the primary reason is that they have fuzzy objectives.

Paul not only had clear-cut objectives, but he also had clear-cut priorities. He not only answered the question "What do I want at the end of life?" but also "What price am I willing to pay for it?"

I happen to be a Van Cliburn fan, and some time ago, a friend who plays in the Dallas Symphony Orchestra said to me, "Howie, are you going to the Van Cliburn concert?"

"I wouldn't miss it!" I said.

"How would you like to meet Mr. Cliburn?" she asked.

"You've got to be kidding!"

"No! You meet me behind the stage at the end of the concert, and I'll introduce you to him."

You can be sure I was there. And I had a question I wanted to ask him. "Mr. Cliburn," I said, "how many hours a day do you spend practicing the piano?"

Very casually he said, "Oh, eight or nine hours a day. Two hours doing nothing but finger exercises."

And to think my grandmother wanted me to play the piano!

Would I like to play the piano like Van Cliburn? You'd better believe it! But not *that* badly.

Often a guy will come to me and say, "Hendricks, I'd give my right arm if I had a marriage like yours."

To which I say, "That's precisely what it may cost you."

I sometimes ask men, "If you had an option—I mean, just one choice—either a great job or a great marriage, which would you choose?" Your priorities enable you to answer that searching question.

In 1 Corinthians 9, Paul said the Christian life is a race—not a hundred yard dash but a marathon. Its success is determined at the end. Paul said it's a unique race because all can win. Not all will, but all can.

But Paul had a fear: He wanted to be sure that "after I have preached to others, I myself will not be disqualified" (1 Cor. 9:27).

If that was a live option to the apostle Paul, what about us?

Where to Find Mentors

Every man reading this book should seek to have three individuals in his life.

You need a Paul.

You need a Barnabas.

And you need a Timothy.

You need a Paul. That is, you need an older man who is willing to build into your life. Please note: not someone who's smarter than you are, not necessarily someone who's more gifted than you are, and certainly not someone who has life all together. That person does not exist. You need somebody who's been down the road. Somebody who's willing to share with you not only his strengths, but also his weaknesses. Somebody who's willing to share his successes and his failures—in other words, what he's learning in the laboratory of life.

Hebrews 13:7 reads: "Remember your leaders, who spoke the word of God to you. Consider the outcome of their way of life and imitate their faith." Please note what you're *not* to imitate: not their method; not their giftedness; not their personality. Comparison is carnality. The Israelite women sang, "Saul has slain his thousands, but David his ten thousands." The comparison to David so embittered Saul that he spent the rest of his life pursuing David rather than the Philistines.

You also need a Barnabas. That is, you need a soul brother, somebody who loves you but is not impressed by you. Somebody who is not taken in by your charm and popularity and to whom you can be accountable.

By the way, don't miss your wife's role in this regard. I've never been able to impress my wife and kids. I tried! I used to think my kids would be impressed that I'm a seminary professor. That's impressive, don't you think? You don't think so? Neither did they.

My younger son once asked, "Hey, Dad, when are you going to get a new job?"

"What's the matter with my job?" I asked.

"I can't explain where you work," he said. "Everyone thinks you work in a cemetery!"

Sometimes I think I do, too!

My kids are not impressed that I studied Greek and Hebrew. They're probably not even impressed that I wrote this chapter for the Promise Keepers! My kids, like yours, are only impressed by the reality of Jesus Christ in our lives.

Have you got anybody in your life who's willing to keep you honest? Anybody who is willing to say to you, "Hey, man, you're neglecting your wife, and don't give me any guff! I know it, everybody else knows it; it's about time you knew it!"

Who's the person in your life who can say, "Hey, man, you talk too much!" without you saying defensively, "Well, I don't see any wings sprouting out on you."

Paul said in Galatians 2:11, "When Peter came to Antioch, I opposed him to his face, because he was clearly in the wrong." That's the kind of Barnabas you need.

Third, you need a Timothy. You need a younger man into whose life you are building. If you want a model, look at 1 and 2 Timothy. Here was Paul, the quintessential mentor, building into the life of his protégé. Notice the issues he addressed. He spoke of the need for somebody who can affirm and encourage you, for somebody who will teach you and pray for you, for somebody who will correct and direct you. That's the kind of person young people are looking for.

Now, how do you get these three men in your life? Let me give you two suggestions. *First, pray that God will bring into your life a Paul, a Barnabas, and a Timothy*. I happen to believe that where prayer focuses, power falls. You may not take God seriously, but He takes prayer very seriously. I am seeing an increasing number of men, younger and older, who are praying for Pauls, for Barnabases, and for Timothys to be brought into their lives. And God is wonderfully answering!

Second, you need to begin to look for these men. Put up your antennae. We have a lot of single students at the seminary who come and say, "Hey, Prof, I'm thinking about getting married."

"Oh," I say, "that's wonderful! You got any gal on the line?"

"No."

"Are you dating any?"

"No."

"Well, how do you expect to find a wife? You think God's going to let her down on a sheet out of heaven?"

Obviously, you've got to become involved in the process. And by the way, don't be surprised if it takes more than one or two experiences before you find that person, because there has to be a personal resonance. There's a chemistry that grows in a good mentoring relationship.

Now, I hear somebody out there saying, "Why are you so excited? You're fairly frothing at the mouth! This mentoring thing really has you." You're right. And it's not because I read some books on mentoring. It's not because somebody came along and said, "Hendricks, here's something else you need to get involved in." No, it's because it's the story of my life.

Remember Walt? Here's what's interesting—I can't tell you a thing Walt ever said. But I can tell you everything about him, because he loved me more than my parents did. He loved me for Christ's sake. And I'm ministering today not only because of a man who led me to Christ and discipled me, but also because he started that mentoring process.

I want to leave you with a passage from Ecclesiastes 4. The wise man says, "Two are better than one." Why?

> Because they have a good return for their work: If one falls down, his friend can help him up. But pity the man who falls and has no one to help him up! Also, if two lie down together, they will keep warm. But how can one keep warm alone? Though one may be overpowered, two can defend themselves. A cord of three strands is not quickly broken. (vv. 9-12)

I want to recommend a cord of three strands—a Paul, a Barnabas, and a Timothy. An older man building into your life, a soul brother to keep you accountable, and a younger man into whose life you can build.

I can assure you after much experience that you haven't lived as a Christian until you have been mentored. And you haven't known fulfillment until you have been involved in the process of mentoring.

Gentlemen of God, go for it!

Strong Mentoring Relationships

by
E. Glenn Wagner

Accepting the mandate for mentoring brings us to the tough part—overcoming the fear and barriers that hinder significant brother-to-brother relationships. I am convinced the benefits of such mentoring far exceed the risks of having to face those fears and barriers.

The Friendless Male

Men have difficulty being emotionally intimate with other men, which hinders the development of friendships. Why is that? The socialization of men and the lack of realistic role models are two significant factors. Here's what we've been taught:

"*Men are self-reliant.*" Men have taken this to an extreme. Typically, we never ask for help, not even when we're lost. We're notorious for going it alone. The Lone Ranger of TV fame kept his mask on and kept mostly to himself—like many men in the church.

"*Men don't feel.*" Actually, men *do* feel, but we have an innate or learned aversion to showing and sharing our emotions. This began when we were young and were told, "Suck it up! Big boys don't cry. Be a man!"

"*Men don't touch.*" Touching, so common to friendships among women, is largely absent among men in our culture, except in contact sports.

"*Men don't need fellowship.*" We tend to be so task-oriented, especially in our business relationships, that we cannot accept an invitation ("Let's do lunch") without asking, "What's up?" or "Why?"

"Men use people, love things." Acquiring things is important to many men. They tend to have relationships of convenience in which they use people to gain wealth and power.

"Men are too competitive." Men are so competitive with each other that enmity, not camaraderie, characterizes most recreational friendships. For many men, the only thing they get emotional about is losing. They buy Vince Lombardi's motto: "Winning isn't everything, it's the *only* thing."

"Men are too macho." On the silver screen and in the news, men who show bravado and violence are defined as "real men." Rarely do the media define manhood in terms of male friendships.

Yet these traditional stereotypes are changing.

The So-called New Man

Many men do desire to share their deepest feelings—but mostly with a *woman* they admire rather than another man in a mentoring relationship. We are told that women like this sort of sensitive and vulnerable friendship, whereas men resist it.

The New Man is described as being sensitive, caring, in touch with his own emotions. He has been disparaged by people on both sides of the gender gap who prefer men to be more macho—in the mold of John Wayne or Sylvester Stallone.

Clint Eastwood used to be on everyone's top ten list of macho men, but now he typifies the new manly man. Eastwood is breaking the mold by taking on male roles that call for more feelings, friendship, even forgiveness. According to reviewers, his movies "Unforgiven" (1992) and "In the Line of Fire" (1993) show us the face of the New Man:

- the steely blue eyes have a softer glint
- the taut jaw muscle is more relaxed
- he reveals some of his softer side—his emotional vulnerability

Nonetheless, the macho male is still the traditional one we were raised with. This causes confusion in the minds of men, and so we wonder: Can a "real man" enjoy a deep and meaningful, nonsexual relationship with another man?

The answer is *yes*. We can and should develop strong mentoring relationships. It won't be easy, however. To break the cultural stereotype and fulfill the biblical mandate to develop man-to-man friendships requires time spent in those relationships. According to George Barna's 1992-93 report, Americans consider friends (relationships) to be most important, yet we spend an ever *decreasing* amount of time with them. Barna wrote:

> Most churches claim they are "friendly." But that may not be enough these days. In a culture where time is always lacking and communication skills are minimal, people may not even know how to go about establishing meaningful relationships with friendly people. The Church has the chance to establish community by offering outlets that create and nurture real relationships.
>
> Small group systems, social events, relational teaching, and modeling relational development are effective methods of providing adults with both the emotional and tangible security they are searching for. (*The Barna Report* [1992-93], pp. 39-40)

The Scriptures give us the mandate for mentoring. Due to the pressures of our culture, many men recognize their need for mentoring relationships. This presents us with a tremendous opportunity. But we must overcome the barriers to friendship. Progress toward that end can be realized in seven steps.

Step 1: *Follow the Golden Rule and Be a Friend*

The Golden Rule applies directly to building strong man-to-man relationships. To find and keep a friend, you must first be a friend. As Jesus said, "Do to others as you would have them do to you" (Luke 6:31). We begin a mentoring relationship by asking ourselves how we like to be treated. The qualities men look for in a mentoring relationship embody one or more of these ideals:

Acceptance—to be fully known, accepted for who I am, without becoming someone's "project."

Understanding—to be listened to without interruption and without unsolicited advice.

Loyalty—to keep confidences without ever wanting to hurt me.

Self-disclosure—to risk revealing innermost feelings without fear of rejection or manipulation.

Availability—to be there for me, night or day, even at 2:30 A.M. in time of need.

Genuineness—for him to be who and what he says he is.

Develop these qualities in yourself and, as like attracts like, you will soon find them in someone else.

Step 2: *Obey the "One Another" Commands of God*

In strong mentoring relationships, we obey what God commands us to do within the Body of Christ. All issues of spiritual growth and maturity are framed in the context of relationships. This is obvious from the many "one another" passages in the New Testament. Here's a sampling:

- *Love one another*:
  "A new command I give you: Love one another. As I have loved you, so you must love one another" (John 13:34).
- *Accept one another*:
  "Accept one another, then, just as Christ accepted you, in order to bring praise to God" (Rom. 15:7).
- *Encourage one another*:
  "And let us consider how we may spur one another on toward love and good deeds. Let us not give up meeting together, as some are in the habit of doing, but let us encourage one another—and all the more as you see the Day approaching" (Heb. 10:24-25).
- *Forgive one another*:
  "Be kind and compassionate to one another, forgiving each other, just as in Christ God forgave you" (Eph. 4:32).
- *Honor one another*:
  "Be devoted to one another in brotherly love. Honor one another above yourselves" (Rom. 12:10).
- *Instruct one another*:
  "I myself am convinced, my brothers, that you yourselves are full of goodness, complete in knowledge and competent to instruct one another" (Rom. 15:14).
- *Serve one another*:
  "You, my brothers, were called to be free. But do not use your freedom to indulge the sinful nature; rather, serve one another in love" (Gal. 5:13).
- *Submit to one another*:
  "Submit to one another out of reverence for Christ" (Eph. 5:21).

The list of "one another" passages goes on, but you get the point. It is impossible for men to fulfill the commands of Scripture without being in significant relationships with one another.

Step 3: *Seize the "Teachable Moments" in Your Life*

Being open to change is another component in building strong relationships with men. As Paul said, "Do not conform any longer to the pattern of this world, but be transformed by the renewing of your mind" (Rom. 12:2).

We cannot build lasting, significant relationships if we are unwilling to change sinful and hurtful attitudes or actions. But take heart; there are many ways to hurdle this barrier. Frequently a "teachable moment" will make us open to such change.

We are most teachable when: (1) struggling in a time of crisis; (2) overwhelmed by inadequacy; (3) confronted with an unresolved need or problem; (4) challenged or measured by a goal; or (5) searching for a more meaningful relationship.

One such teachable moment contributed significantly to the formation of a mentoring relationship for a Wisconsin Promise Keeper. As he tells the story:

> I was due to be married in June but got cold feet and called it off one month before the wedding. My career in life insurance sales was also at a dead end. I had asked Dick, a seminary professor and sometime mentor over the years, to officiate at the wedding. Wanting to comfort me in my disappointment and guide me in my ongoing search for meaningful work, Dick came out from Boston to Wisconsin on the weekend the wedding would have happened.
>
> As we shared heart to heart, Dick ended up inviting me to write for him. I changed careers to apprentice myself as a "Timothy" to this veteran communicator of the faith. That mentoring relationship has continued to this day, but it would not have begun had it not been for a crisis of confidence 15 years ago.

Teachable moments do not have to be life-changing experiences like that one to catapult you into a mentoring relationship, however. You just have to be open to change and acknowledge your need.

Step 4: *Acknowledge Your Need of Others*

Until you acknowledge your need for the gifts, talents, and perspectives of other men in your life, you will never pursue positive, nurturing relationships.

Some years ago, while pastoring in New Jersey, I reconnected with a former college professor who had been a real encouragement to me. In the course of our phone call, I invited Stan to come and preach at my church. To hear him preach and watch the congregation respond so positively was great. Even greater were our times of "catching up."

That's when I began realizing my need for this mentor in my life and ministry. When I suggested the possibility of regular talks, prayer, and accountability with Stan, he was humble and honest enough to voice his need for me. Even though we have been called to minister in different states and must content ourselves with only a rare get-together, I have yet to come away from one of our monthly phone calls without feeling affirmed.

By acknowledging their need for each other, two men can make a positive impact on their respective lives, ministries, and families.

Step 5: *Accept and Appreciate Differences in Others*

We acknowledge our need for others by placing a high value on their opinions and ideas, even (and especially) when they differ with us. Differences of culture, gifts, talents, temperaments, and physical abilities should all be valued with the special, unconditional love that Christ bestows on us.

After my move to Denver, Colorado, I continued to acknowledge my need to connect with other men of like heart. However, I had not been able to get beyond the acquaintance stage in any relationship. Then I followed the advice of an out-of-town friend and met Rod, who was teaching at a local seminary. Within minutes, I knew Rod was someone I could relate to, enjoy, learn from, grow with, and be held accountable to on important matters. But I also wondered if such a relationship was possible. How could two men so unlike each other grow together?

Our differences are obvious. I'm white; he's black. I was raised in suburbia; he was raised on a farm. My path took me through the rebellion of the late '60s and early '70s; he went through college and on to seminary, then graduate school—all with a positive focus and unswerving direction. We both love golf, but he often hooks his ball, and I often slice mine. We both love to preach, but our styles are so different. We both love to laugh, yet my humor is mostly in side comments, while his involves storytelling accented by hearty laughter.

Those very differences, however, are what make our relationship special and powerful. I have learned from Rod's personal pain; as he has grown through it, so have I. Thanks to our differences, I have a deeper appreciation for what is important in life.

Step 6: *Devote Yourself to People*

The very thing we're trying to develop and maintain—a mentoring relationship—could be jeopardized by shifting our focus and devoting ourselves to goals, programs, or tasks. When that happens, men are viewed as a means to an end rather than as an end in themselves. To remedy that, involve yourself in the lives of men quite apart from how they fit into your business agenda.

Devotion to people begins with a focus on your own family. You are the only husband or father they have. You may find it somewhat natural to develop mentoring relationships at work, with a built-in expectation for training and developing younger associates. When you intentionally invest in someone younger and bring him along with you, you multiply or generate your talents through others.

All the above-stated principles of developing and maintaining man-to-man friendships apply to a men's small group. This last step in building mentoring relationships may also be the first.

Step 7: *Band Together in Small Groups for "PPP"*

When pairs of men in strong mentoring relationships band together for mutual edification, support, and accountability, you have a small group of Promise Keepers. Conversely, existing small groups are an excellent source of brother-to-brother friendships that could develop into mentoring relationships.

Assuming you are committed to keeping your promises and will take the risk of being a friend—even if that means caring enough to confront—you are ready to band together with other men and make mentoring relationships happen on a small-group scale.

Coach Bill McCartney, founder of Promise Keepers, has a handy way of remembering the basic agenda of men's small groups. He calls men together for "PPP," which stands for prayer, pages (of Scripture), and pain.

- *Prayer* is conversing with God—acknowledging His supreme place in our lives, giving thanks for all things, and bringing the needs of others and ourselves before the One who can do something about them.

- *Pages* of Scripture are what we use to find out more about God and His provision for us. The divine-human encounter is life-changing. Referring to Scripture as the final arbiter in all matters of faith and practice keeps us from merely pooling our ignorance or giving unsubstantiated advice.
- *Pain* is our reason for going to prayer and Scripture in the first place. Men are most genuine with one another when they are vulnerable and share their pain—in their marriages, with their children, or at work—with each other.

Handle Conflicts with Care

Despite the best of intentions, conflicts will arise in most friendships and small groups. In such times, you find out who your real friends are. Conflicts are neutral; it's how you react that makes—or breaks—the friendship. Here are some pointers for handling conflicts constructively.

- *Give others the benefit of the doubt*. Rather than always looking for a hidden agenda, trust people to keep their word and live up to their agreements.
- *Double check your own attitude*. Assert your opinion and don't be defensive, but do defend the other person's right to speak his mind and hold an opinion different from yours.
- *Separate people from the problem*. Go soft on people, hard on issues—that is, love people more than opinions.
- *Focus on interests, not on positions*. Do not bargain over the substance of a position, but do build on common interests, which are vested in maintaining the relationship.
- *Invent creative options* for mutual gain. Go for a win-win solution to the conflict by broadening the range of options and agreeing on objective criteria or principles by which you will decide what's best.
- *Compromise on matters of taste or personal convenience*. Stand firm with integrity, however, on matters of principle or personal values.

Confrontation and Care

A balance between confrontation on issues and care for people will strengthen and lengthen any mentor relationship. Many men in Scripture model this tough love. It was used, for example:

- by the prophet Nathan with the adulterous David (see 2 Sam. 11–12);
- by Jesus with Peter, who had denied his Lord three times (see John 21:15-19);
- by Paul with Peter, who had compromised on the issue of justification by faith for Jews and Gentiles alike (see Gal. 2:11-16).

This need for honest confronting of issues with genuine caring for people is made practical for mentors in the following chart (adapted from David Augsburger, *Caring Enough to Confront* [Ventura, Calif.: Regal, 1980]).

Confronting	Caring
I feel deeply about the issue at stake.	I care about our relationship.
I want to clearly express my view.	I want to hear your view.
I want respect for my view.	I want to respect your insights.
I want you to trust me with your honest feelings.	I trust you to be able to handle my honest feelings.
I want you to keep working with me until we've reached a new understanding.	I promise to stay with the discussion until we've reached an understanding.
I want your unpressured, clear, honest view of our differences.	I will not trick or pressure you, nor will I manipulate or distort the differences between us.
I want your caring-confronting response.	I give you my loving, honest respect.

Remember that the Bible commands both the one who has been offended and the one who did the offending to seek reconciliation. Acknowledge whatever actions and attitudes on your part led to the break in the relationship. Admit the hurt and consequences to the people involved, as well as remorse over the offense itself. Yet the repentant person cannot restore himself; someone else must take the initiative.

Barnabas (see Acts 4:36) was noted for his ministry of restoring broken people. He took the government agent Saul under his wing, defending him when Saul was newly converted and the early church did not yet trust him. On another occasion, years later, Barnabas sided with the young John Mark, who had suddenly dropped out of the missionary team and was rejected by Paul (see Acts 15:36-41). Thanks to a mentoring relationship with Barnabas, John Mark later proved useful to Paul (see 2 Tim. 4:11).

You get the point. Mentoring relationships are not for the faint-hearted. But those who go the extra mile and show biblical love will reap the rewards. Restoring a brother may be the toughest job a mentor has to do. However, only a mentor—one who has proved his faithfulness as a friend—will be trusted at those critical, teachable moments that make or break a man's ministry.

Conclusion

You can be a Barnabas to a Saul and a John Mark. Or you can be a Paul to a Peter and a Timothy. In either case, follow the mentor's creed (2 Tim. 2:2): "The things you have heard . . . in the presence of many witnesses [your Barnabases] entrust to reliable men [your Pauls] who will also be qualified to teach others [your Timothys]."

The mentor's creed, coupled with the mandate for mentoring, is essential to being a Promise Keeper. We need a few trusted brothers to help us keep our promises. That's all there is to it. It's that simple. And it's that hard.

A Man and His Mentors
Personal Evaluation

Can you identify one or more of the following in your life?

a Paul ________________

a Barnabas ____________________

a Timothy ___________________

For each of the people above for which you do not have a name, can you think of any *potential* candidates?

In the Group

1. If you're comfortable doing so, share with the group the prayer you wrote out in the past week.
2. Complete this statement: When I think of mentoring, I . . .
3. In 60 seconds, tell about someone who was (or is) a mentor in your life.
4. Dr. Wagner identifies several reasons men have difficulty forming close friendships. As a group, review the list and discuss which you feel are most accurate in your experience:
    - Men are self-reliant.
    - Men don't feel.
    - Men don't touch.
    - Men don't need fellowship.
    - Men use people, love things.
    - Men are too competitive.
    - Men are too macho.
5. Relate how each of you did in identifying a Paul, a Barnabas, and a Timothy in your life. To help discussion, you might answer the following questions:
    - What characteristics am I looking for in my Paul?
    - What characteristics do I want in a Barnabas?
    - What characteristics should I look for in a Timothy?
6. How can we be brothers/mentors to each other?
7. Consider getting together as a group for a social activity—a barbecue, a round of golf, a softball game with your kids, or something similar.

Memory Verse: "Though one may be overpowered, two can defend themselves. A cord of three strands is not quickly broken" (Eccles. 4:12).

On Your Own

1. List potential candidates for a Paul, a Barnabas, and a Timothy in your life. Begin praying for God to match you with the right man/men in each of these areas.
2. Read Promise 3, "A Man and His Integrity," before the next meeting.

PROMISE 3

A Man and His Integrity

A Promise Keeper is committed to practicing spiritual, moral, ethical, and sexual purity.

PROMISE 3

Introduction

If we are living out the first two promises—to honor Christ and to build vital relationships with a few men—it should be evident in our lives. That's what this third promise is about. Promise Keepers are known as men of integrity.

What does integrity look like? That question can be answered by seeing how our faith affects the way we conduct our business and the moral choices we make. It's integrity that prevents a Promise Keeper from entering into a shady business deal. It's integrity that says he will choose to express his sexuality only within the confines of his marriage. It's integrity that makes him do the right thing instead of just the easy thing.

Three men help us sort through the issues inherent in this commitment. First, Dr. Tony Evans takes on spiritual purity. If a man's outward actions are an expression of his inward being, then we become men of integrity by first becoming pure in spirit. Dr. Evans is senior pastor of Oak Cliff Bible Fellowship in Dallas Texas, president of Urban Alternative ministries, and chaplain of the Dallas Mavericks basketball team.

Dr. Gary Oliver then leads us into the area of moral and ethical purity. Gary is clinical director of Southwest Counseling Associates in Denver. He has written several books, including *Real Men Have Feelings Too*.

Finally, Jerry Kirk deals with probably the central cultural issue of our age: our sexuality. Jerry is president of the National Coalition Against Pornography.

Spiritual Purity

by
Dr. Tony Evans

What is now a worldwide phenomenon is painfully apparent in the United States. America is losing its families. Current statistics, the news media, and my own pastoral counseling experience drive that point home with disturbing force. Since a culture's only hope of survival is its families, our very existence is threatened as home after home falls victim to divorce, abandonment, abuse, or neglect.

For years, sociologists have argued over the causes of the problem. Politicians have thrown billions of dollars into our cities, hoping that would solve the riddle. Others have stood by, scratching their heads, wondering where society went wrong. In the meantime, the negative statistics soar and the lives of countless children are irreparably damaged.

I am convinced that the primary cause of this national crisis is the feminization of the American male. When I say *feminization*, I am not talking about sexual preference. I'm trying to describe a misunderstanding of manhood that has produced a nation of "sissified" men who abdicate their role as spiritually pure leaders, thus forcing women to fill the vacuum.

In the black community, for example, women run the show to an alarming degree. Sixty percent of black children grow up without a father in the home. By the turn of the century, that figure will climb to 70 percent. When those children are sent off to school, 83 percent of their teachers will be women.

If they are fortunate enough to be involved in church activities, virtually all of their Sunday school teachers, caregivers, and other leaders will be women. And even in the white community, where more fathers are in the homes, the declining influence of men is a serious problem.

Please don't misread me. It is proper—in fact, essential— for children to be nurtured, guided, and cared for by women. But God neither designed nor endorsed the kind of exaggerated imbalance we see today. In many cases, women are forced to shoulder the leadership load alone and carry responsibilities that God never intended them to bear. (After all, if the men won't do it, *someone* must.) In the process, their emotional and physical circuits are being overloaded.

The blame for this eclipse of masculine influence must be laid at the feet of the feminized male. Somehow, many men got the idea that the definition of manhood has to do with how many women they have conquered and the number of children they have sired. Somebody told these entrepreneurs of pleasure that sex without love or commitment is appropriate today. As a result, in 1985, taxpayers spent $16.5 billion to take care of children with mothers but no fathers.

Both men and women are enslaved by this completely nonbiblical and nonhistorical understanding of manhood. In the meantime, much has been said about liberating women, when what we really need are *men* who are liberated from the distorted images conjured up by our corrupt culture.

Many of these misconceptions are created and sustained on the movie screen. In their "generosity," movie moguls have given young boys the chance to choose from an assortment of role models. Heading the list are "heroes" like Rambo and Dirty Harry, along with characters portrayed by Steven Seagal, Arnold Schwarzenegger, Jean Claude van Damme, and Chuck Norris. These guys leap into danger with the courage of Superman, catch bullets between their teeth, and challenge armies single-handedly. When the smoke clears, they emerge unharmed, stepping over the bodies of their foes.

These "macho men" pull in big bucks at the box office. Evidently, it isn't difficult for a two-dimensional piece of fiction to compete with a missing or disinterested father. This helps explain why you've got kids carrying guns and gangs going to war as they emulate the only "fathers" they have ever known.

Given time to fester, this absence of leadership degenerates into a loss of conscience. After all, Rambo is not only violent, but he's also uncaring; he'll blow you away in a heartbeat and never give it a second thought. We run the risk of spawning a generation of sociopaths. A person with a conscience can be reached. You can talk with him about right and wrong—or at least deter him with the threat of severe consequences. But a person without a conscience is completely out of control.

More and more juvenile offenders aren't intimidated by parents, police, or prison. In fact, there's a growing sentiment among our young men that jail isn't such a bad option. After all, on the "inside," you are guaranteed three meals a day, a warm bed to sleep in, an indoor commode, and the opportunity to hang out with the boys. If detention is no longer a deterrent, traditional approaches to law enforcement are little more than a grim joke.

At the other end of the media spectrum are the men of prime-time television, models of undisciplined males who live by their hormones rather than by principles of dignity, moral purity, and respect. Far too many men are functioning like dogs—living simply to satisfy their lusts, no matter what the cost to themselves, others, or society at large.

As reason gives way to fear, people look for a place to pin the blame. In a Ted Koppel TV special on juvenile delinquency, accusing fingers were pointed at the criminal justice system, an unfair economy, and persistent racism. While each of those issues is worthy of our attention, they are all symptoms of a more serious disease. Let's face it! Economics is no excuse for promiscuity and irresponsibility. And racism doesn't get teenage girls pregnant.

The fact is, if Dad doesn't provide spiritually responsible leadership in the home, baby is in big trouble. That's what the folks downtown don't understand. Without strong families built on a framework of biblical morality, there is no sum of money—no federal, state, county, or municipal program—that can get us out of the ditch we've fallen into.

How do we break the cycle? By getting men to assume their responsibilities and take back the reins of spiritually pure leadership God intended us to hold. Otherwise, our culture is lost. I believe ours is the last generation capable of making a difference. After this, it will be too late. We must become real spiritually directed men once again, pure in our passions and our priorities.

The Bible provides us with a portrait of such a man. His name was Job. We remember him as the man whose faith was tested so severely. But here, we will see quite another view of this biblical patriarch.

The Character of a Spiritually Pure Man

Job is set forth as the epitome of a spiritually pure man. God says that he was "blameless, upright, fearing God and turning away from evil" (Job 1:1, NASB, as are all scriptures in this chapter).

In Job 29, his character is described in more detail, giving us a clear guide for any man who wishes to understand the comprehensive nature of spiritual purity.

First, a spiritually pure man has divine continuity with the past.

> Oh that I were as in months gone by, as in the days when God watched over me; when His lamp shone over my head, and by His light I walked through darkness; as I was in the prime of my days, when the friendship of God was over my tent; when the Almighty was yet with me, and my children were around me. (Job 29:2-5)

Job could look back over his shoulder and see the divine movement of God in his past. He had a divine heritage. Somewhere along the way, we lost touch with that. No longer does God sit in control over what happens in our communities. Christian principles of living are not passed from generation to generation as they once were. I suggest that this process started grinding to a halt when fathers began *sending* their children to church instead of *taking* them; when fathers gave up on providing spiritual leadership in the home.

Job, on the other hand, had a different agenda:

> And it came about, when the days of feasting had completed their cycle, that Job would send and consecrate them [his sons], rising up early in the morning and offering burnt offerings according to the number of them all; for Job said, "Perhaps my sons have sinned and cursed God in their hearts." Thus Job did continually. (Job 1:5)

Here was a man with ten children! How easy it would have been to argue that he was too busy and too tired to pray. Instead, however, he spent his early mornings on his knees, bringing his family before the Lord. He understood that a father is to be the priest of his home and maintain that continuity of commitment between generations by setting a godly example.

Second, a spiritually pure man is committed to raising children.

Notice the reference in our original text: "My children were around me" (Job 29:5). Job wasn't showing up at the tent after the kids went to sleep. Nor was he rushing them to bed just to get them out of his hair. He let his kids *surround* him—*all ten of them*. When it comes to transferring our values to our children, much more is *caught* than *taught*. The process requires a father's time—a commodity that seems to be in dangerously short supply these days.

In Job's age, it was understood that parenting involved a commitment not only to quality, but also to quantity. The biblical approach to family planning is quite simple: The more children, the better. The way to build a nation (or, in our case, to change a community) was by multiplication of families. How different from the selfish world we live in today, where children are thought of as a drain on our energy and resources. "I've got to have my two Cadillacs, can't afford kids." "Got to have my house in the suburbs, can't afford kids." "Got to have my Armani suits, can't afford kids." That, frankly, is a pagan, sissy way of thinking.

Third, a spiritually pure man earns respect.

Earning respect is very different from simply expecting it. A real man behaves in such a way that you have no choice but to respect him.

> When I went out to the gate of the city, when I took my seat in the square; the young men saw me and hid themselves, and the old men arose and stood. The princes stopped talking, and put their hands on their mouths; the voice of the nobles was hushed, and their tongue stuck to their palate. (Job 29:7-10)

Job went to the gate of the city (that's downtown) and sat in the square (the city council). The young men saw him and said, "We've got to go. Mr. Job is here!" Can you see our inner-city teenagers facing a situation like that? No, they'd say, "I ain't gettin' up for no Mr. Job. Ain't nobody gonna tell me what to do!"

Once, older men and women were treated with kindness and respect. Now they are seen as easy prey, helpless victims. If young people don't learn to respect their own fathers, why should they extend that consideration to a stranger?

The older men, on the other hand, rose when Job came on the scene. Though these fellow council members were his elders, Job commanded their respect.

The princes were the "yuppies," the smooth talkers cutting business deals on their way up the ladder of success. When Job walked in, they stopped talking. Job changed his environment by being part of it. Without saying a word, he set a new standard, much as a clergyman does today. The tone of a conversation often changes when a representative of the Lord listens in: "Shh! It's the reverend."

This phenomenon isn't limited to those in the ministry. But it certainly won't take place if you're participating in the "cussing and fussing." Why should anyone follow your lead if they've heard you using perverted language, running down the dignity of women, and generally dishonoring God?

Fourth, a spiritually pure man is also a man of mercy.

> I delivered the poor who cried for help, and the orphan who had no helper. The blessing of the one ready to perish came upon me, and I made the widow's heart sing for joy. (Job 29:12-13)

Mister, they lied to you if they told you big boys don't cry. Real men have enough compassion to recognize and respond to the pain of others. They don't feel the need to hide or deny those tender feelings, and they have the courage to act on behalf of those weaker or less fortunate than themselves. They are involved in their community, making a difference for the have-nots of this world.

Job used his riches to resolve problems, not to elevate himself above the level of "common people." Job's benevolence may have shut the mouths of the proud nobles, but the widow's heart sang for joy. When poor folk saw Job, they saw their champion. Job knew how to make his caring count.

Fifth, a spiritually pure man is a person of justice.

> I put on righteousness, and it clothed me; my justice was like a robe and a turban. I was eyes to the blind, and feet to the lame. I was a father to the needy, and I investigated the case which I did not know. (Job 29:14-16)

A real man knows that wrong is wrong. You can't influence him by pointing out that the crowd is heading in the opposite direction. He will seek out the truth and react accordingly. He isn't intimidated by race or by riches. He refuses to play political games.

Sissies trade in truth for popularity. They'll sell their souls for acceptance. By the thousands, they join gangs in the vain hope of finding the love, attention, and self-esteem they failed to find at home. Gangs are "alternative families" made up of cynical, hard-bitten, resentful youth who never learned right from wrong—because Dad wasn't there to teach them.

Sixth, a spiritually pure man is a man of stability.

> Then I thought, "I shall die in my nest, and I shall multiply my days as the sand. My root is spread out to the waters, and dew lies all night on my branch." (Job 29:18-19)

My father is getting old now, and I love him more than ever. He still lives in the same neighborhood in Baltimore where I grew up, but the place has changed. You can't walk the street without seeing a drug deal going down on the corner. Every year when we visit, I say, "Dad, I'm really worried. You can't stay here. It's getting too dangerous."

He tells me, "My roots are here. I've raised my children and served my Lord, and I want to spend the rest of my years with my wife *right here*. God has taken care of me up until now. Why would He stop?"

That is stability. That's a man who knows what God has called him to do, and you can depend on him to do it. Families today lack roots because they lack purpose and direction. They jump from place to place, job to job, looking for the good life. Their plans for the future are a muddle of self-centered whims. A real man may be on the move (like Abraham), but his family knows where he's going, and they can draw strength from his dependability.

Finally, a spiritually pure man has wisdom.

> To me they listened and they waited, and kept silent for my counsel. After my words they did not speak again, and my speech dropped on them. And they waited for me as for the rain, and opened their mouth as for the spring rain. I smiled on them when they did not believe, and the light of my face they did cast down. I chose a way for them and sat as chief, and dwelt as a king among the troops, as one who comforted the mourners. (Job 29:21-25)

You don't need a college education to be wise. The world is full of well-educated fools. Real wisdom is the ability to take God's truth and apply it to life. All it requires is a heart for God and some plain old common sense. "If any of you lacks wisdom, let him ask of God, who gives to all men generously and without reproach, and it will be given to him" (James 1:5).

Reclaiming Your Manhood

I can hear you saying, "I want to be a spiritually pure man. Where do I start?"

The first thing you do is sit down with your wife and say something like this: "Honey, I've made a terrible mistake. I've given you my role. I gave up leading this family, and I forced you to take my place. Now I must reclaim that role."

Don't misunderstand what I'm saying here. I'm not suggesting that you *ask* for your role back, I'm urging you to *take it back*. If you simply ask for it, your wife is likely to say, "Look, for the last ten years, I've had to raise these kids, look after the house, and pay the bills. I've had to get a job and still keep up my duties in the home. I've had to do my job *and* yours. You think I'm just going to turn everything back over to you?"

Your wife's concerns may be justified. Unfortunately, however, there can be no compromise here. If you're going to lead, you must lead. Be sensitive. Listen. Treat the lady gently and lovingly. But *lead!*

Having said that, let me direct some carefully chosen words to you ladies who may be reading this: *Give it back!* For the sake of your family and the survival of our culture, let your man be a man if he's willing. Protect yourself, if you must, by handing the reins back slowly; take it one step at a time. But if your husband tells you he wants to reclaim his role, let him! God never meant for you to bear the load you're carrying.

Men, you can minimize your wife's skepticism by taking some immediate and visible steps in the right direction. For example, let your schedule reflect your new commitment. "Honey, instead of watching Arsenio Hall (substitute the program of your choice), we're going to turn off the TV, and that's going to be our talk time." Or, "Instead of going to the gym five days a week, I'm cutting back to three, and I'm going to save every Friday night for you. We're going to start dating again."

Another area that deserves immediate attention is church. Stop making your wife set the spiritual tone for your household. Assume the task of getting your family to church, and behave like a leader when you get there. Reclaim teaching the boys in Sunday school. Reclaim the roles of deacon and leader. Become surrogate fathers to the fatherless. Be a churchman. Allow yourself to become accountable to other men who, like you, want to be God's kind of man.

A third way to demonstrate your resolve to lead is by becoming a biblical lover. Biblical love is commitment love. It has more to do with your actions than with your feelings. Any dog can satisfy his libido. It takes a really spiritually pure man to be faithful *regardless* of his passions.

Near the top of the "Ten Most Stupid Statements" list is this gem: "I don't think God wants us miserable, and *together*, we're miserable." Of course God doesn't want you miserable; but He doesn't want you apart, either. Many couples simply don't recognize or won't consider the third option: honoring your commitment to each other and working on the problems.

That idea doesn't go over very well these days. The "me first" mentality is too dominant. After all, even Burger King lets you have it your way. But that kind of attitude doesn't come from the Bible. It originates with the sissies on the street corner who say, "Your old lady makes you go home? Man, I go home whenever I want to go home. Ain't no woman gonna tell *me* when to go home." Of course, that explains why he's on the street corner. If his wife has any sense, she doesn't want him at home!

Stop listening to the maladjusted meddlers. A real man armed with biblical love sacrifices anything that interferes with his calling as a husband, father, and churchman. You owe your family and your God nothing less.

If you've failed in the past, confess your sins to God. Then recommit yourself to your spiritual priorities. Get back on your feet, dust yourself off, and "*go and sin no more*."

What I've presented in these pages is bound to be unpopular. I'm prepared for that reaction. My only request is that you ask yourself some questions. Of course, the most important is, "Is this concept biblical?" If so, the opinions of my critics mean little. The next question is, "Does it apply to me?" Not every man has become feminized. If you're genuinely free of the symptoms I've described, we desperately need your help to carry the message to others. But if you're unsure—if you've squirmed in your chair or felt the hairs on the back of your neck stand on end during the past few moments—take time to pray. Ask the Lord to help you evaluate your performance as a father and a husband.

The stakes are too high to let false pride stand in our way. At risk are our children, our families, our nation, and our future.

Come on, men. We've got work to do.

Black-and-White Living in a Gray World

by
Gary J. Oliver, Ph.D.

The judge looked down from his bench and, in a somber voice, declared, "Mr. Wilson, this is your day of reckoning!" Then he sentenced him to seven and one-half years in federal prison.

In response, Wilson's lawyer requested that he be allowed a few minutes with his family and friends before surrendering to the authorities.

The judge replied, "Mr. Wilson is going to be taken by the marshals right now. You should have thought of that before."

Wilson was one of four California men convicted of financial fraud and sentenced to prison in that particular case. *Five* men were originally investigated, but the fifth, Mark Jacobs, was not arrested and charged.

Jacobs had been invited to join the financial scheme by four friends (the men sent to jail) in a weekly Bible study. They had assured him their plan was totally legal. Yet something inside him said it wasn't right. While it was hard to say no to good friends, he chose to go with his conscience and tell them he wouldn't participate.

The lawyers for the four convicted men pleaded with the judge that their clients had simply made mistakes of poor judgment. They were good men who loved their wives and kids, gave to charities, and were active in their churches. Their crime involved a "gray" area, crossing a line that wasn't clear.

The judge disagreed. "It is not hard to determine where the line is," he said. "The guy who drew the line is Mark Jacobs. He knew what was right and what was wrong, and he didn't hesitate. Hopefully, now we will have fewer people who are willing to walk up to the line and dabble with going over the line. We will have people like Mr. Jacobs who wouldn't touch this thing with a ten-foot pole."

That case is just one example of the moral and ethical crisis sweeping our nation. While the cast may change and involve stockbrokers, bankers, lawyers, or television evangelists, the script is the same. We are a generation that isn't sure where the line is between right and wrong. Many don't believe there is a line, or, if there is, they don't care.

In 1966, an American professor named Joseph Fletcher published an influential book called *Situation Ethics*. His basic premise was that there is nothing that's universally good or bad, right or wrong. There are no absolutes. Morals are determined by the situation. An act that is right in one situation may be wrong in another.

What was only a philosophical discussion in 1966 has become, in 1994, the basis for morals in our society. Thirty-five years ago, our country followed the Judeo-Christian ethic. Few people questioned that chastity was a good thing, that hard work was the duty of every responsible man, that homosexual conduct was wrong, and that it was never right to lie, cheat, steal, or commit adultery. But today, our ethics and morals are no longer based on Jerusalem; they're based on Sodom and Gomorrah.

If you take situation ethics to its logical conclusion, you end up with Auschwitz, Dachau, and Buchenwald. In fact, at the entrance to the Auschwitz concentration camp is a sign with Adolf Hitler's words: "I want to raise a generation devoid of conscience." He almost succeeded.

Every day, we're influenced by the philosophy and values of those around us. In a famous experiment, some students put a frog in a container of water and began to heat the water slowly. The water finally reached the boiling point, yet the frog never attempted to jump out. Why? Because the changes in the environment were so subtle that the frog didn't notice them until it was too late.

As Christian men, it's easier than we think to end up like the frog. Many godly men—pastors, seminary professors, respected and beloved Christian leaders—have yielded to the world's values because they failed to discern the subtle changes occurring around them. Before they knew it, they were in hot water. They didn't want that. They didn't intend to get there. They didn't think it could happen to them. But it did.

If the desire of your heart is to be a Promise Keeper, you need to think seriously about the connection Jesus made between Christianity and morality. Who we are should determine what we do. The Bible commands us to become "holy and blameless" (Eph. 1:4), to "live a life worthy of the calling you have received" (Eph. 4:1), to be "mature" (Eph. 4:13) and "imitators of God" (Eph. 5:1).

What do you think of when you hear the word *holy?* Most of us think of someone else, not ourselves. In both the original Hebrew and Greek of the Bible, the word *holy* refers to something or someone separated and set apart for God. A major characteristic of a holy man is purity. Something that is pure is spotless, stainless, containing nothing that does not properly belong, free from moral fault or guilt.

Purity isn't an accident, and it doesn't just happen overnight. Peter compared it to the process of purifying gold (see 1 Pet. 1:6-7). Gold has to be heated and reheated several times for the alloys and impurities to be brought to the surface, where the goldsmith can remove them. If you forget that becoming pure is a process, you risk becoming overwhelmed by discouragement when you experience those inevitable setbacks.

Still, it's not enough that you desire to be pure, nor will sincerity or hard work necessarily get you there. You also need a plan to "be conformed to the likeness of his Son" (Rom. 8:29). As the ancient saying goes, a journey of a thousand miles begins with the first step. What will be your first step? Where can you begin? The rest of this chapter presents seven simple steps that God can use to help you move beyond good intentions and down the path to purity.

Step 1: *Make a decision.*

When Babylon's King Nebuchadnezzar conquered Judah, he ordered thousands of the best and brightest young men to be taken as captives to Babylon. His goal was to immerse them in the seductive culture of Babylon and thus remake their character. He would turn their hearts from the God of their fathers to the idolatry of the Chaldeans.

Daniel was one of those men. The king changed his name to Belteshazzar, which means "a servant of the god Bel." Then the king ordered the captives to go through three years of special training, which included a certain diet. That's where Daniel drew the line. He couldn't avoid the king's education, but he could refuse food that had been offered to idols. In Daniel 1:8, we read that "Daniel resolved not to defile himself with the royal food and wine."

Daniel made a *decision* not to compromise and defile himself. Webster defines *defile* as "to make unclean or impure, to corrupt the purity or perfection of, debase, sully, taint, dishonor, contaminate, pollute, dirty, soil, poison, smear, blot, blur, smudge, stain, tarnish, profane, infect, dishonor, or disgrace." That's not a pleasant list of words. Daniel chose to stand tall for what he knew to be right. The influence of social morality was nothing. Being God's man was everything.

Almost every day, you come to some kind of fork in the road. Like Daniel, you face tough choices. What you decide at that fork is greatly influenced by the choices you made the day before about the kind of man you are.

Step 2: *Choose to put first things first.*

It's not easy to be pure in an impure world. Even if you become a cultural ostrich and avoid all movies, listen only to Christian radio, and read only Christian books and magazines, you are still going to struggle. You will never become a godly man by negation. A pure, pollution-free environment doesn't make pure people. In Mark 7:15, 20-23, Jesus made it clear that what's *inside* a man defiles him. That's where we need to start.

If a farmer doesn't plant seed in the ground, he will never harvest a crop. It doesn't matter how weed-free his ground is; he must also plant and cultivate good seed. In the same way, we can only reap a harvest of purity and integrity by planting the good seed of God's Word into our lives. I'm not talking about merely reading the Bible. I'm talking about allowing the Holy Spirit to plant the truths of Scripture deep into our hearts and minds through consistent Bible reading and memorization, meditation, and prayer.

To be effective, truth must be planted in our hearts daily. After 35 years of being a Christian, I'm convinced that the best time to do this is in the morning. Keep in mind that this is being written by someone who is *not* a morning person. However, a statement by the late Dietrich Bonhoeffer greatly challenged this reluctant morning person:

> The entire day receives order and discipline when it acquires unity. This unity must be sought and found in morning prayer. . . . The morning prayer determines the day. Squandered time of which we are ashamed, temptations to which we succumb, weaknesses and lack of courage in work, disorganization and lack of discipline

> in our thoughts and in our conversations with other men, all have their origin most often in the neglect of morning prayer. . . . Temptations which accompany the working day will be conquered on the basis of the morning breakthrough to God. (*Psalms: The Prayer Book of the Bible* [Minneapolis: Augsburg, 1970], pp. 64-65)

Step 3: ***Determine where the line is, and then stay a safe distance behind it.***

Most Christian men want to be strong and victorious. We want to hear God say, "Well done, thou good and faithful servant." We want our lives to be characterized by integrity. The problem is that each of us has blind spots, weaknesses, and deeply entrenched habits that can sabotage our best intentions.

We need to move beyond the biblical absolutes and determine what kinds of things are healthy for us and what kinds are unhealthy. What one man can watch or listen to with no problem may open the door to unnecessary temptation for another man and increase his vulnerability to sin. Satan's first step in the battle for our minds is to distract us (see James 1:14-15). The distraction itself may not be sin. It may seem small and insignificant. However, whatever distracts us or weakens our resolve puts us at risk.

To help determine your line, honestly answer these questions:

- In what areas of your life do you consistently struggle?
- Are there any particular sins to which you are consistently vulnerable?
- Do any activities consume too much of your time?
- Over the past years, what has been Satan's most effective "bait" to attract you?

Moral failure is rarely the result of a blowout; almost always, it's the result of a slow leak. For some men, it starts with the healthy desire to provide for their families, and they end up becoming workaholics, driven by an insatiable appetite for more. For other men, it starts with something as seemingly innocent as lingering too long over the swimsuit issue of *Sports Illustrated* or the latest *Victoria's Secret* catalogue.

Look at Samson. He was physically strong and attractive, born of godly parents, and appointed to be a judge in Israel. He had everything going for him. Yet he never drew a line and dealt with his tendency toward lust. For that he paid a heavy price.

Determine where the line is. If it's not something that is clearly spelled out in Scripture, pray about it and seek the counsel of several wise friends. Once you've decided where the line is, *walk ten yards back and make that your line!* Always leave yourself a margin. Don't see how close you can get to the line without going over. That's like a scuba diver seeing how little air he can leave in his tank and still get to the surface. Only a fool would do something like that.

Step 4: *Guard your heart.*

Jesus made it clear that we can't serve two masters. Where our treasure is, there will our hearts be also (see Matt. 6:21). As Chuck Swindoll wrote,

> The quest for character requires that certain things be kept in the heart as well as kept from the heart. An unguarded heart spells disaster. A well-guarded heart means survival. If you hope to survive the jungle, overcoming each treacherous attack, you'll have to guard your heart. (*The Quest for Character* [Portland, Ore.: Multnomah, 1987], pp. 19-20)

Only the passionate love of purity can save a man from impurity. When Jesus met Peter on the seashore after His resurrection, He didn't bawl him out for his lack of faith in denying Him. Three times He asked Peter the simple question, "Do you love Me?" A growing affection for our Lord Jesus Christ is the only antidote for the kind of apathy that leads us down the primrose path to compromise.

Step 5: *Guard your mind.*

There's a large railroad switchyard in St. Louis. One switch that begins with just the thinnest piece of steel directs a train away from one main track and onto another. If you follow those two tracks, you'll find that one ends in San Francisco, the other in New York.

Our thought life is a lot like that switch. The seemingly simple choice of what we set our minds on can determine the outcome of our spiritual warfare. Just a small deviation from God's standard can put us at risk and lead us far afield from our desired destination. Someone once said:

> We have never said or done an ungracious or un-Christlike word or action that was not first an ungracious and un-Christlike thought. We have never felt dislike or hate for a person without first of all thinking thoughts of dislike that have grown into hate. We have never committed a visible act of sin that has

> shamed us before others that was not first a shameful thought. We have never wronged another person without first wronging that person in our thoughts. What we habitually think will, sooner or later, manifest itself clearly in some visible expression of that thought.

The mind is the place where decisions are made for or against the truth. What we choose to read, watch, and think about will determine, to a great degree, whether we will be victims or victors, conquered or conquerors.

Step 6: Guard your eyes.

In Genesis 39, we see that Joseph was smart enough to know you can't play with fire and not get burned. Job also knew the importance of guarding his eyes. He wrote, "I made a covenant with my eyes" (Job 31:1). David, however, lingered too long, stared a bit too much, and unwisely entertained unhealthy fantasy. He didn't guard his eyes and ended up committing adultery with Bathsheba and murdering her husband.

The little Sunday school song has some powerful wisdom for us:

> Oh, be careful little eyes what you see.
> Oh, be careful little ears what you hear.
> Oh, be careful little lips what you speak.
> There's a Father up above, looking down in tender love,
> Oh, be careful little eyes what you see.

Step 7: Guard the little things.

Jesus said that "whoever can be trusted with very little can also be trusted with much" (Luke 16:10). As a young man, I didn't understand why that was so important. Now I know that in the process of becoming a godly man, there are no "little" things. In fact, how we handle the seemingly little things determines, over time, our response to the big things.

If you allow one thought or activity in your life that you know is not best for you, even though it may not be sinful in itself, you will find that your spiritual eyes will become darkened, your spiritual ears hard of hearing, and your soul numb to the "soft promptings" of the Spirit. Beware of the temptation to justify or rationalize. Many of my own failures started by moving in a direction my head rationalized by saying, "It isn't sin," but my heart said, "Don't do it." Be on guard for statements such as, "It's not that bad," "I've seen worse," or "The Bible doesn't have anything to say about that." Don't ask what's *wrong* with a certain behavior or choice; ask what's *right* with it. Ask, "Is what I'm considering more likely to move me closer to or further away from my goal of being a Promise Keeper?"

If there is any hope for our marriages, our families, our cities, our nation, and our civilization, we men must passionately embrace the biblical standard for who God would have us to be and to become. It's not enough to give mental assent to truth. We must make a commitment to be men who aren't afraid to count the cost and then stand tall—at times seemingly alone, but in truth with thousands of other men who want to make their lives count.

Remember: "Blessed—happy, enviably fortunate, and spiritually prosperous—are the pure in heart, for they shall see God" (Matt. 5:8, Amp.).

God's Call to Sexual Purity

by
Jerry Kirk

Let's be honest! Sexual purity is not easy, whether you're a seasoned believer or a new follower of Christ.

John is typical of many men I've known. At age 14, having been raised in a home with strong Christian values, he had his first exposure to pornography. He found a seemingly harmless soft-core magazine that someone had thrown away on the street.

Fascinated and aroused, John began to consume more and more pornography. It hooked something deep inside him. He started looking for harder, more bizarre material when the soft-core magazines began to seem less arousing. By the time John turned 17, he was addicted and frequenting porn stores, which never bothered to check his age.

At 19 he married, but he continued to feed on the pornography that had become a constant in his life. Soon it was the model for intimacy with his wife, and before long he was forcing her to act out things he had seen in the magazines.

After seven years, John's first marriage was destroyed. He quickly found another wife, but he was still convinced he didn't have a problem, and his consumption of pornography escalated. Before long—discouraged, frustrated, and feeling worthless—his second wife filed for divorce.

John's story is not unusual. I've heard numerous similar accounts from earnest Christian men at Promise Keepers in Colorado and elsewhere across the country.

The sad fact is that one is hard pressed to find any encouragement for a life of sexual purity in our modern culture. Billboards, magazines, and television use sex to sell everything from autos to cologne, featuring ever-more-explicit messages as the ability of old approaches to grab attention wears off. Movies, radio "shock jocks," and other media openly and continually encourage infidelity and promiscuity. Many policymakers take it as a given that young adults will be sexually active and consider it futile to encourage abstinence. American men, *including many Christians*, spend upwards of $8 billion a year on hard- and soft-core pornography.

If the surveys are to be believed, over a third of all men cheat on their spouses. Our culture's rates of divorce, out-of-wedlock pregnancy, sexually transmitted diseases, and devastated relationships each bear witness to the prevailing sexual ethic and the consequences of abandoning God's call to sexual purity.

I paint this rather dark picture as a way of noting that apart from God's Word, your family, and other Christian men, you will receive little encouragement from the culture surrounding you to live a pure life. But for the Promise Keeper who desires to follow Christ, *there is hope!* I haven't told you the full story of John. Stay with me, for there is wonderful news for the man who chooses to live according to Christ's call to purity and with *genuine, lasting* relationships. That's the rest of the story!

Why Does Sexual Purity Matter to God?

Choosing to let Jesus be Lord of your sex life will shape *every* other area of your life, because sexuality is at the center of our being. This decision will influence your current and future ability as a husband, father, and Christian. Choosing purity is difficult, but for those who put in the hard work and prayer, living by Christ's standard is a road to deep joy and *real* sexual satisfaction. At no time in history has our society been more in need of men willing to stand up, be different, and demonstrate the joy of living by a fundamentally better standard.

Purity, in its essence, is a reflection of God's character and presence in our lives. To the extent that we live in sexual purity, we reflect for the whole world that God is at work within us, shaping our desires, choices, and actions with more than just hormones.

This matters to God because it goes to the very heart of our witness, our understanding of God's faithfulness, and the vital issue of whether we really believe God when He tells us a given course of action is better for us. It matters to God because He deeply loves us and wants us to enjoy that which is most fulfilling and meaningful. Practicing sexual purity, even though it's hard, is also one of the most accurate reflections of the depth of our relationship with Christ.

We expect God to keep His promises to us, particularly His promise to forgive our sins because of Christ. We live in the firm hope that what He has promised is really true. *Yet many men find it difficult to believe God has their best interests at heart with respect to sex.* Some Christian men consider God's call to sexual purity a cross they must somehow bear rather than a great blessing to be enjoyed because it enriches marital love and family life. In calling us to be sexually pure, God asks us to model His faithfulness to His people (see Eph. 5:29-32). When we cross the boundaries set by God for our well-being, we choose a path that, while sometimes pleasurable in the short run, undermines our confidence in God and says to Him that we don't really believe He knows what's best for us.

With respect to our witness to the world, we need only look at the numerous examples of believers who have not trusted Christ in this area. How do you feel when a well-known pastor or Christian leader is found at the local pornographic bookstore or in an adulterous relationship? Do you have more or less spiritual respect for the advice of a friend whose sexual conduct is out of control or a young Christian leader who is involved sexually with his girlfriend? Sexual failure devastates our witness, because the world understands all too clearly that God has a different standard and that we're not living by it. If we close off this area to Christ's control, our integrity is compromised, and His lordship is emptied of meaning.

What Does Sexual Purity Encompass?

Our sexuality and desires are a wonderful gift from God, and He knows they can best be enjoyed in the context of sexual purity—in both thought and action. It is vital to remember that sexual intimacy is *pure* in the truest sense only when exercised appropriately. While writing an encouraging letter to a friend is a good thing, it is not appropriate while driving down a busy highway during rush hour. Circumstances do matter, even for good things, and this is particularly so with our sexuality.

For the single man, this means a willingness to wait until marriage for sexual intercourse. God's call to virginity before marriage is unequivocal. For those who have made a mistake already, it means making a commitment today to a "secondary virginity" that will wait for your spouse. When our repentance is sincere, God can and will forgive and restore us from *any* sin. It is never too late to begin obeying God and enjoying the fruits of faithfulness.

Purity also means obeying Jesus' command not to lust after that which is not ours (see Matt. 5:27-28). This is tough! It means not putting ourselves in a position to use women sexually either by thought or by action (e.g., pornography is an exploitive form of mental intercourse). For the single man, it means treating every woman he dates in a manner that respects and preserves her purity for her future husband. Purity also means seeking to follow Christ's call in spirit, not just by the letter of the law. It does *not* mean trying to find a thin line marking the boundary of what's acceptable and crawling right up to the edge (and maybe even peering over a few times).

For us married men, sexual purity means reflecting God's absolute faithfulness to us in our faithfulness to our wives. Adultery can take many forms. Watching racy movies on a business trip in an airport hotel, with or without masturbation, is a form of emotional adultery that will eventually weaken the marriage. Every man faces this challenge when he travels alone overnight. Real intimacy is not just a function of sex—it permeates our lives only when emotional, spiritual, and sexual faithfulness characterize our relationship with our spouses.

Living a Life of Sexual Purity

God has set a high standard, albeit one that will bless us and those we love. Here are some key principles many men have found helpful in their effort to keep this essential promise:

- *Past mistakes don't mean future failure!*

Few if any Christian men are without some sexual sin. Because none of us fully understand the depth of God's love for us, few have been totally faithful. But a mistake in the past is no reason to give up practicing sexual purity. The God who can redeem and bless every other area of our lives can also take control of our sexual being. Confession and forgiveness can cleanse. Even if this is the third or fourth time we're starting down this path—or even the tenth or one hundredth time—*it's still worth the effort.*

- *Sexual purity is as much a matter of the mind as it is of the body.*

Paul's words in Romans 12:1-2 are the key:

> Therefore, I urge you, brothers, in view of God's mercy, to offer your bodies as living sacrifices, holy and pleasing to God—this is your spiritual act of worship. Do not conform any longer to the pattern of this world, but be transformed by the renewing of your mind. Then you will be able to test and approve what God's will is—his good, pleasing and perfect will.

If our bodies are to be a living sacrifice to God, we must start by being "transformed by the renewing of your mind." Physical sexual sin is usually the result of allowing sinful thoughts to take root in our minds and hearts. How many of us have nourished thoughts of sexual unfaithfulness in our fantasies, only to later find them difficult to resist? If we surround ourselves with titillating images, pornography, and other suggestive media, we will find it impossible to practice sexual purity. If we control what goes into our minds, purity will be much easier. As the psalmist noted, "How can a young man keep his way pure? By living according to your word. . . . I have hidden your word in my heart that I might not sin against you" (Ps. 119:9,11).

- *Practicing sexual purity is a process as well as a commitment.*

Our commitment to sexual purity requires development over time. It must be cultivated like any other godly habit or it will not be there when temptation comes. Joseph fled without his cloak rather than sin against God with Potiphar's wife (see Gen. 39). His ability to do so was a function of doing the right thing again and again so that he was ready when tested. We should walk with both a bedrock commitment to certain standards and a constant humble understanding that, but for the grace of God, we would not be able to stand firm.

- *Don't pretend your desires don't exist.*

Denial does no more to produce healthy sexuality than hedonism. God created us as sexual beings, and our desires are normal. We need to channel them in productive, God-given directions.

I was once emotionally unfaithful to my wife while counseling a woman for an extended time in a former congregation. It could have destroyed my marriage. But God recaptured my attention and clarified the seriousness of the situation. I was led to immediately turn from that friendship and avoid all further counseling with the woman. I then told my wife, facing up to my sin, and we worked through the issues together. In addition, I called two trusted friends and asked them to keep me accountable. I needed God's help, and I needed those brothers.

A word of caution is in order here. I don't recommend that every man confess every detail of every sexual sin to his wife. That can be more harmful than helpful. It may bring relief to the man but put a terrible, unbearable burden on the wife.

Any decision about confessing a sexual sin to one's wife should be made in light of these questions:

- How would I feel if she were confessing these things to me?
- Have we shown grace to each other in smaller failures?
- Are my humility and repentance genuine? Am I following the biblical model of real confession and asking for forgiveness? ("Will you forgive me? I know I don't deserve it, but I'm asking for it.")
- How much detail is it necessary to reveal so my confession is real and her forgiveness can be complete? (Details are likely to stick painfully in her mind.)
- Is the timing right? Do we have unhurried time to listen and talk through the issues?

Experience with more than 100 men has shown me that when there is genuine repentance and God's grace is part of both spouses' lives, it is most helpful to face the truth together at the foot of the cross. Jesus is able to forgive and to help us forgive each other.

- *No substitute exists for personal accountability with other godly men.*

In seeking to practice sexual purity, we do well to remember that sin is seductive for the believer and unbeliever alike. We need to surround ourselves with a few men who are close friends and eager to follow Christ. Then we can learn together, hold one another accountable to a godly standard, and confess our sins to one another. Secret sins have much more power and usually last much longer than those we acknowledge to our brothers. And together we can grow in our commitment to and practice of purity.

- *Understand the importance of sexual purity to our marriages, families, and heritage.*

Our faithfulness gives strength to our wives. Their deepest needs include affection, communication, trust, security, and confidence in our fathering. All of those are undermined by sexual and emotional unfaithfulness. But when we fortify our wives by our faithfulness, we strengthen their ability to give themselves to us and to our children. We also strengthen our children by our example.

• *Understand the importance of sexual purity to our Christian witness.*

Nothing undermines our influence more than sexual failure. We must work on purity not only for our own well-being and joy, but also for the health of the church.

• *Understand the importance of sexual purity to our own sexual fulfillment within marriage.*

When we experience sexual intimacy, in God's design, we are yoked to the other person in a unique way. The two become one spiritually and emotionally when they become "one flesh." Thus, a man brings to his marriage bed every woman with whom he has ever had intercourse. Each can affect his ability to wholeheartedly and singlemindedly love his wife and enjoy true and unique intimacy with her. I have never met a man who waited until marriage for sexual intimacy and then regretted the choice. But I've met hundreds who regretted their premarital sexual encounters.

For the Traveling Man

Here are some practical suggestions for dealing with the lonelinesss and anonymity of the road without forfeiting your purity:

1. Decide *beforehand* not to consume pornography. Most mistakes are made when you haven't resolved to avoid the material prior to leaving home. Tired, alone, and unknown, it's easy to slip into destructive lust.
2. Whenever possible, stay with friends while traveling by yourself. Many businessmen who travel often develop significant friendships in other cities. If you're around others, you're less likely to fall into temptation.
3. When you stay in a hotel, request at check-in that the staff block the pornographic movies from your room. If you make this decision up front, you'll face much less temptation. (It's hard to call back down to the front desk and ask that they *send* such movies to your room.) In addition, you should offer a polite but firm word of protest at every hotel that carries those movies. It will strengthen you, and if enough men do it, the hotels might stop showing them.
4. Choose specific things you want to see and do before settling in for the night. A phone call home is very helpful. If you develop a game plan and fill your time with productive uses, you'll be less tempted.

5. Make a habit of reading Scripture before turning on the TV. Some passages to use: Psalm 101:2-4; Romans 12:21; 1 Corinthians 6:18-20; Ephesians 6:10-17; James 4:17.

The Rest of John's Story

I introduced John at the beginning of this chapter. Now let me tell the rest of his story.

When his second wife filed for divorce, he finally began to face the ruinous consequences of pornography in his life. Accepting that he had a problem was the first, most important, and most difficult step for him. Then John committed his life to Christ, knowing he couldn't conquer the problem on his own. Next, because he couldn't yet bring himself to discuss his addiction with a group, he went to talk with his pastor. After confessing his sin and his pain, he asked for guidance and accountability. The pastor agreed, and John started on the road to recovery.

John's wife, seeing his courage in finally confronting his problem, withdrew her request for a divorce.

It has now been 13 years since John committed his life to God's higher and better standard. He keeps in close touch with other Christian men who continue to encourage him and hold him accountable. Freed from pornography all these years, John has seen all his relationships blossom.

One is sometimes hard pressed to distinguish the sexual behavior of Christian men from that of nonbelievers. As a Promise Keeper, you have the opportunity to bless your own life, your family's life, and the witness of the church by demonstrating that there's a better way to live. Our culture is ripe for change as it deals with the ruin, loneliness, and devastation left by the sexual revolution. Make a commitment today to be among those men who will lead the way to renewal.

A Man and His Integrity
Personal Evaluation

Read each of the following statements, and rate yourself on a scale from 1 to 10, with 1 being "I totally disagree" and 10 being "I totally agree."

1. I consider myself a spiritually pure man in the model of Job. _____
2. I know where my line is—that is, where I'm in danger morally—and I am ten steps behind that line._____
3. My affection for Christ is well-protected. _____
4. My thought life is well-controlled. _____
5. My eyes will not wander where they should not go. ______
6. I am faithful to do what is right even with "the little things." ______
7. As for sexual purity, that area of my life is totally under control. ______

Now look over the list and select the one with the lowest rating. What one thing could you do this week to move that area closer to a 10?

In the Group

1. Briefly describe your reaction as you read through the chapters about this promise (e.g., frustrated, intellectual agreement, convicted, encouraged, etc.) and why you felt that way. (Each member should do this.)
2. Complete the following sentences: As a boy, I thought that being holy meant . . . In light of these last three chapters, I now think it means . . .
3. When I think of a man of integrity, I think of . . .
Explain why.
4. Take some time to talk about an area of temptation that is frustrating to you. (Remember that temptation by itself is not sin and that we're all tempted.)
5. Complete this sentence: When Gary Oliver talked about getting too close to the line, I thought of . . . What can you do that will help you back off several steps from that line?
6. Review the suggestions at the end of Jerry Kirk's chapter on sexual purity. Realizing this may or may not be an area your group is ready to open up about, at least talk about those ideas. Are they reasonable and doable? Are you willing to be accountable to this group about this area the next time you travel?

7. James 5:13,15 says, "Is any one of you in trouble? He should pray. . . . If he has sinned, he will be forgiven." If anyone feels he would be helped by confessing a past sin, he may do so now so the group can pray for him. Close by praying for each other in the group, perhaps using the information given in response to questions 4 and 5.

Memory Verse: "For we do not have a high priest who is unable to sympathize with our weaknesses, but we have one who has been tempted in every way, just as we are—yet was without sin. Let us then approach the throne of grace with confidence, so that we may receive mercy and find grace to help us in our time of need" (Heb. 4:15-16).

On Your Own

1. From the personal evaluation above, faithfully carry out the activity you identified that would move your lowest-rated area closer to a 10.
2. Read Promise 4, "A Man and His Family," before the next meeting.

Promise 4

A Man and His Family

A Promise Keeper is committed to building strong marriages and families through love, protection, and biblical values.

PROMISE 4

Introduction

A man in the latter stages of his life often reflects on how he has lived. And as has been noted, few men ever express regret that they didn't earn more money or work longer at the office. But many state bitterly that they should have paid more attention to their families. A little more time spent working on the marriage, a few more hours spent with their children during the formative years, and maybe things would have turned out better.

You don't need to experience such regret. A commitment now to give your family its rightful priority can make a world of difference in years to come. No one will ever know whether you could have worked a few more hours or earned a few more dollars. But your wife and children will care deeply if they feel neglected.

Two men share a passion to help men do something about their families *now*. Gary Smalley is renowned for his easy-to-understand principles for family harmony. As president of Today's Family, he speaks, writes, and teaches around the world, helping families function as God intended. In his chapter, he will reveal five time-tested secrets that can revitalize your marriage.

Then Dr. James Dobson gives powerful insight into the importance of fathering, including the ultimate priority. Dr. Dobson is a noted psychologist and best-selling author heard daily on the "Focus on the Family" radio broadcast. His chapter is excerpted from his book *Straight Talk*.

Five Secrets of a Happy Marriage

by
Gary Smalley

If I could convey only one message to men, the contents of this chapter would be it.

As I've traveled the world ministering to families, I've noticed five things consistently displayed among couples with healthy, vibrant marriages and families. As I tell you about my friends the Brawners, see if you can identify the five elements in their home.

The Brawners are a normal family—not perfect by any means. They've got their shortcomings, and they've got their strengths. But if I knew you were living with your wife and kids the way Jim is with his, I would be very encouraged about the direction of our world.

Jim and Suzette Brawner live in a small town in Missouri and have three children: Jason, who's 19 at the time of this writing, a national swimming champion and a freshman in college; Travis, their 17-year-old son who's an outstanding three-sport athlete in high school; and Jill, their beautiful and talented 13-year-old. Jim and Suzette are in their early forties. Jim came from a home that had dysfunctional elements. But he realized that while his background could lead to unhealthy behavior in his own marriage, he could do something about it. He has worked hard to build a strong marriage and to raise, with Suzette, three emotionally healthy children.

Recently Jason came home for the first time from college. He was unusually nervous because, as part of his initiation into the swim team, he had been coerced into wearing an earring. None of the men in his family had ever worn an earring, and it just wasn't done among their circle of friends. Jason felt the roof might come off when Mom and Dad saw him.

Jason pulled into the driveway and found his mom. She was so excited to see him that she gave him a big hug before she noticed his ear and gasped. Then she laughed. "What a great joke!" she said. "I assume it's one of those stick-on kinds?"

"No, Mom, this is the real thing," Jason answered. "I had my ear pierced. Everybody on the swim team has an earring, and I was the only one who didn't, so I gave in."

Suzette became nervous, not because she was upset with her son, but because she wondered how her husband would react when he got home. After taking Jason's laundry and getting him something to drink, she called two friends. Then, while Jim was still at work, she made a trip to the home of one of those friends and discussed how she should handle the situation.

Both Jason and his mother were anxious as Jim arrived home.

When he walked in the door, Jason said, "Hi, Dad, I'm home for the weekend."

Jim immediately hugged his son—on the side opposite the earring—then said, "Well, how's college going?" He hadn't noticed, and Jason just kept waiting for the explosion. Finally, Dad saw it. "Hey-y-y, what's this?" he said.

Jason thought, *Oh, no! He's going to rip it off my ear.*

Suzette gently suggested, "Now, don't overreact."

But Jim didn't react at all. Calmly and sensitively, he asked, "What's going on?"

Jason answered, "Dad, everybody on the swim team has an earring. I knew you'd be upset, but Dad, I was the only guy who didn't have one. The seniors said either I do it or, you know, I'm in trouble."

"If you want to wear the earring, that's your business," Jim answered. "It's not up to me. Only God knows how much I love you. Personally, I wouldn't wear an earring, but hey, I understand the pressure you were getting."

Suzette calmed down immediately. "I thought you were going to be mad," she told Jim.

"No, we need to support our son," he said. "Actually, I'd like to do something about it, but I don't think anything would help."

While they were in the middle of that discussion, my wife, Norma, and

I showed up. We're a part of the Brawners' support team. Along with three other couples, we meet weekly in a small group, plus we meet socially and pray for each other. The Brawners know about our family and everything that goes on, and we know the same about their family.

My wife gave Jason a big hug and said, "That's a good-looking earring."

Then I gave him a hug and asked, "How's the temperature in the house today?"

He had an embarrassed smile on his face as he said, "So far, so good."

So what's the big deal about this ordinary family conflict? What the Brawners did is what I wish millions of families would do. Even though they may seem small, this brief encounter contained all five qualities that are extremely important.

Five Qualities of Healthy Couples

In many respects, that was a typical family conflict. What's not so typical is the way the Brawners handled it. Did you catch the five things Jim and Suzette did in their relationship and family? They aren't all immediately obvious, but all were definitely there and operational.

They had a clearly defined menu of expectations.

They understood and used meaningful communication.

They were involved in a small support group.

They recognized their personal, emotional wounds and had learned how to compensate for them.

They were dependent on the Lord Jesus Christ for their quality of life.

In any family, one thing you can count on is crisis. It may be a child having poor grades or breaking up with a friend. It may be the disappointment of not making an athletic team. It could be a major event, such as a long-term family illness or a job change that forces the family to move across the country. Whatever the issue or crisis, those five things the Brawners have will hold the family together and greatly increase the likelihood that your marriage will thrive.

Let's look more closely at each of the five elements and see how we can use them in our own marriages and families.

1. Healthy couples have a clearly defined menu of expectations.

When you go to a restaurant, you look at a menu, and you expect to be able to order anything you want from it. The owners know that if they provide good food and service, you'll come back.

The same is true in a successful home. When a family agrees, preferably in writing, on a menu of options for quality life and relationships, they will enjoy a healthy, successful family. Here is just a sample of things you might consider putting on your menu:

Honor for your loved ones. Honor means "to place a high value on." It's the decision we make that someone has great worth. From that decision and God's power comes our ability to genuinely and consistently love others.

You can determine that each member of your family is highly valuable and to be honored. You can do that by first honoring God, then building security into your wife and your children by verbally praising them and protecting them.

A *plan for dealing with unresolved anger*. Scripture admonishes us to not let the sun go down on our anger (see Eph. 4:26). Every family needs a healthy process for resolving anger and keeping it low. Jim and Suzette could have let anger erupt when they saw Jason wearing an earring. Instead, they dealt constructively with their emotions and honored their son.

Activities that foster emotional bonding. You can't just sit at home and talk every day. You need to do things together outside your home that will draw you together.

Many other areas can be covered in your family's menu. They should be agreed upon together during periods of calm. Some resources in the back of the book will help you develop your menu.

2. Healthy couples understand and practice meaningful communication.

Picture yourself driving through a fast-food restaurant. You pull up to that little speaker box and announce, "I'd like two hamburgers, two fries, an onion ring, and two Diet Cokes."

After a moment, you hear from the speaker, "Did you say a hamburger and a cheeseburger, two fries, an onion ring, and two Cokes?"

You clarify, "No, I didn't say that. I said *two* hamburgers, two fries, an onion ring, and two *Diet* Cokes."

In a similar way, I recommend that couples practice "Drive-Through Talking." Take the time to repeat back to one another what you think you heard your partner or your children say. It's very honoring and meaningful.

Within marital and family communication, it's important to remember that you're always trying to move toward the deepest level of intimacy. Healthy families are connected emotionally, spiritually, psychologically, and physically. They feel two big things: They feel connected, and they feel safe in that connection—they can say things and feel they're not going to get rejected or belittled.

Experts have identified five levels of communication, and healthy families operate on all five levels.

The shallowest level is when you just use clichés like "Hi." "How are you?" "Did you have a good day?" "Is everything going Okay?" "Give me five." Clichés are little phrases that have little meaning. They're pretty safe. You can say them and know you're not going to get in trouble.

The second level of communication is when you relate facts. "Did you see in the paper today. . . ?" "It looks like it's going to rain tomorrow." "Do you think the Dodgers [or your home team] are going to win?" "The football team doesn't seem that good this year."

The third level of communication is riskier, and a lot of couples, especially when they're starting out, are hesitant to go to it because of potential conflicts. It is the stating of opinions: "I think this is going to happen," "I believe this is the way things ought to be," or "We ought to have a date one night a week."

Whenever you state opinions, you increase the possibility of conflict. That's a good time to use drive-through talking and repeat back what you think you hear your mate saying until you achieve clarity and understanding. Keep in mind that conflict with your mate or your children is healthy and normal. What's not healthy is walking off and not talking about it, or else reacting, getting angry, and dishonoring each other. But handled properly, conflicts are doorways to intimacy. They open up the last two areas of communication.

The fourth level is expressing and understanding each other's feelings. This can best occur when you feel safe.

Not long ago, Norma and I went on a short trip with the Brawners. In the driveway before we left, Suzette said to Jim, "I feel so nervous about leaving Travis [their 17-year-old] home alone the first week of two-a-day football practices. Who's going to cut the watermelon for him at six in the morning? Who's going to make his breakfast? Who's going to have his sandwiches ready? I just feel so uncomfortable. Isn't Travis going to feel he's been abandoned?"

Suzette felt safe expressing those feelings. But that openness can be shattered when we're insensitive. Without thinking, Jim said, "Come on, Suzette, will you relax? We've got to take vacations once in a while. Let the kids grow up."

Then he realized what he was doing, and he stopped attacking his wife's feelings. He hugged her and said, "I see you're really hurting, and that's okay. Should we cancel the trip?"

"No, I want to go. It's just hard," she said.

We men need to understand that in healthy homes, everyone feels free to express feelings without fear of hearing "That's stupid!" "Only an idiot would feel like that," or "Why don't you grow up?" Maybe the feelings are immature, but they're real nonetheless. It's not our job to analyze; it *is* our duty to love, value, and understand our mates and our children.

The fifth and deepest level of communication is when we feel safe in revealing our needs. I can say I need a hug. I can say I need to hold and kiss my wife and be involved sexually. Or she can say she needs to go shopping and ask if I'll go with her.

Norma and I were talking recently as we prepared to fly to Colorado to speak at a physicians' conference. She had learned there was going to be a western dinner on Friday night, so she had bought a western outfit. She brought it home and said, "I need to have you look at this outfit I bought. What do you think?"

In the past, I might have said, "Hey, I'm busy. Can I do it later?" Or I would have looked at the outfit and said, "What difference does it make? Just buy it if you want it."

But I have learned that such words are dishonoring. So I looked at my wife and said something like, "I love the outfit! It makes you look younger." (Most men know from experience that that's something women like to hear.)

Then she said, "I don't have a coat to go with it. But I found one at this outlet mall, and I really like it. I need you to go look at it with me and tell me what you think."

Norma hasn't always felt free to reveal her needs to me. I used to be very controlling, rigid, critical, and prone to giving lectures. The damage I did in the first few years of our marriage still lingers. But I want her to feel increasingly safe, because then I know we're going to go increasingly deep in our intimacy.

3. Healthy couples are associated with a small, healthy support group.

I suggest you meet regularly with three—at the most four—other couples who have the same commitment to God and their marriages that you have. In a healthy group, each person feels the freedom, safety, love, and commitment to think out loud. In fact, group members want you to think, reason, and grapple with important issues.

An effective support group is built on deep friendship. Members give each other hugs and affection when needed. They do things together like camping or dining. But they also have a definite purpose for meeting every week. It may be to study a marriage book or to discuss ways to improve their parenting skills. Whatever the purpose, it must be specific if the group is to stay on course. The weekly meeting is not a gossip session. It's not a time to criticize your pastor or other church members. And it's definitely not a time to put down your mate. Sure, every once in a while, someone's going to slip, but you can't have a steady diet of that. There must be freedom to feel and think and discuss your feelings and needs with each other.

Why are support groups so important? First, they give you power to make the changes we all need to make to stay healthy. There's a dynamic that takes place where you actually experience energy from someone else hugging you and saying things like "We can do this together," "I know you're in conflict, but it will get better," and the all-important words, "We love you."

Second, you get the tremendous power of accountability, knowing that once a week you're going to ask each other "How's it going?" in the area of your purpose for meeting together. You know you're going to have honesty, so when you say it's not going well, someone will ask, "What are you doing about it? What steps are you going to take to make this better?"

Third, if you come from an unhealthy home, a good small group gives you a chance to be reparented. You get to see how couples can interact in a healthy way. That leads to the next area of strong family life.

4. Healthy couples are aware of unhealthy or offensive behavior stemming from their heritage.

The Bible says that the sins of a father are visited on the children up to four generations. So some of the things I'm doing to my wife and children today could be directly related to my great grandfather, his behavior and offensive ways toward my grandfather, then my father, and so on down the line. Now, that doesn't mean I'm to blame my great grandfather or my father. But it helps to *understand* who I am so I can take 100 percent responsibility for my life today and do whatever is necessary to raise a new generation that God will bless.

What you need to do is to look at your life and ask, "Did I come from an unhealthy environment?" You might rate your parents on a scale from 0 (not at all) to 10 (all the time) in such areas as the following:

- ___ were like dictators, demanding obedience
- ___ were rigid, forceful, with strict rules, values, beliefs, and expectations
- ___ were critical, judgmental, with harsh punishment
- ___ were closed to talking about certain subjects like sex, religion, politics, feelings
- ___ were poor listeners to my thoughts and feelings
- ___ used degrading names like "stupid," "lazy," or "no good"

The higher the score, the more potential there is for an unhealthy relationship in your home. Based on your score, you may need some specific help from a counselor to analyze where you came from and develop a plan for healing.

Unlike a lot of couples, Jim and Suzette Brawner understand the families they came from and the strengths and weaknesses they inherited. They struggled in their marriage until Jim got some help. Now he's in charge of a small-group ministry called "Homes of Honor," and through it he gives couples training to overcome past mistakes and to gain support for the changes they want to make.

5. Healthy couples have a vibrant relationship with Jesus Christ.

Norma and I, Jim and Suzette, and many other couples have entered into a relationship with Jesus Christ in which we are dependent on Him as our primary source of abundant life. That life includes love, peace, joy, patience, kindness, and self-control. The Holy Spirit gives us the spirit of completeness, or contentment, so we don't have to struggle and look for anybody else to get our needs met.

The apostle Paul wrote, "My God will meet all your needs according to his glorious riches in Christ Jesus" (Phil. 4:19). He also wrote that we can know the love of God "that surpasses knowledge—that you may be filled to the measure of all the fullness of God" (Eph. 3:19).

Over and over, the Bible talks of how Jesus is our life and that we're not to have any other gods, nor are we to look to anything else as our source of life. Everything else—wives, kids, cars, homes, jobs—is overflow to the relationship we have with Him. When that permeates our relationship as husband and wife, we experience what Scripture calls a calm or quiet spirit. We're relaxed because we know that Jesus filters everything that comes into our lives. Plus He can take any trial we experience and, as He said in Isaiah 61:3, turn that sorrow into gladness. Our kids will tend to pick up that spirit and follow in our footsteps as long as they're not angry with us.

Do you have a home like Jim and Suzette's, where there's a clear menu of expectations and communication is open and goes deep in the five levels toward intimacy? Do you recognize problems from your childhood, and do you have a support group to help you grow as a couple? And finally, do you recognize Jesus Christ—not your wife, family, job, or anything else—as the source of life?

I suggest that, with your wife, you rate your marriage in each of those five areas on a scale from zero to ten. Then choose one of the five and talk about how you can move it closer to a ten. That will put you on the road to a healthier and more rewarding marriage.

The Priority of Fathering

by
Dr. James C. Dobson

I was walking toward my car outside a shopping center a few weeks ago, when I heard a loud and impassioned howl.

"Auggghh!" groaned the masculine voice.

I spotted a man about 50 feet away who was in great distress (and for a very good reason). His fingers were caught in the jamb of a car door which had obviously been slammed unexpectedly. Then the rest of the story unfolded. Crouching in the front seat was an impish little three-year-old boy who had apparently decided to "close the door on Dad."

The father was pointing frantically at his fingers with his free hand, and saying, "Oh! Oh! Open the door, Chuckie! They're caught . . . hurry . . . Chuckie . . . please . . . open . . . OPEN!"

Chuckie finally got the message and unlocked the door, releasing Dad's blue fingers. The father then hopped and jumped around the aisles of the parking lot, alternately kissing and caressing his battered hand. Chuckie sat unmoved in the front seat of their car, waiting for Pop to settle down.

I know this incident was painful to the man who experienced it, but I must admit that it struck me funny. I suppose his plight symbolized the enormous cost of parenthood. And yes, Virginia, it is expensive to raise boys and girls today. Parents give the best they have to their children, who often respond by slamming the door on their "fingers"— especially during the unappreciative adolescent years. Perhaps that is why someone quipped, "Insanity is an inherited disease. You get it from your kids."

Without wanting to heap guilt on the heads of my masculine readers, I must say that too many fathers only *sleep* at their homes. And as a result, they have totally abdicated their responsibilities for leadership and influence in the lives of their children. I cited a study in my previous book *What Wives Wish Their Husbands Knew About Women* that documented the problem of inaccessible fathers. Let me quote from that source.

> An article in *Scientific American* entitled "The Origins of Alienation," by Urie Bronfenbrenner best describes the problems facing today's families. Dr. Bronfenbrenner is, in my opinion, the foremost authority on child development in America today, and his views should be considered carefully. In this article, Dr. Bronfenbrenner discussed the deteriorating status of the American family and the forces which are weakening its cohesiveness. More specifically, he is concerned about the circumstances which are seriously undermining parental love and depriving children of the leadership and love they must have for survival.
>
> One of those circumstances is widely known as the "rat-race." Dr. Bronfenbrenner described the problem this way, "The demands of a job that claim mealtimes, evenings and weekends as well as days; the trips and moves necessary to get ahead or simply to hold one's own; the increasing time spent commuting, entertaining, going out, meeting social and community obligations . . . all of these produce a situation in which a child often spends more time with a passive babysitter than with a participating parent."
>
> According to Dr. Bronfenbrenner, this rat race is particularly incompatible with fatherly responsibilities, as illustrated by an investigation in the 1970s which yielded startling results. A team of researchers wanted to learn how much time middle-class fathers spend playing and interacting with their small children. First, they asked a group of fathers to estimate the time spent with their one-year-old youngsters each day, and received an average reply of fifteen to twenty minutes. To verify these claims, the

> investigators attached microphones to the shirts of small children for the purpose of recording actual parental verbalization. The results of this study are shocking. The average amount of time spent by these middle-class fathers with their small children was thirty-seven seconds per day! Their direct interaction was limited to 2.7 encounters daily, lasting ten to fifteen seconds each! That represented the contribution of fatherhood for millions of America's children in the 1970s, and I believe the findings would be even more depressing today. (*What Wives Wish Their Husbands Knew About Women* [Wheaton, Ill.: Tyndale, 1975], pp. 157-58)

Let's compare the 37-second interchanges between fathers and small children with another statistic. The average preschool child watches between 30 and 50 hours of television per week (the figures vary from one study to another). What an incredible picture is painted by those two statistics. During the formative years of life, when children are so vulnerable to their experiences, they're receiving 37 seconds a day from their fathers and 30 or more hours a week from commercial television! Need we ask where our kids are getting their values?

Someone observed, "Values are not *taught* to our children; they are *caught* by them." It is true. Seldom can we get little Johnny or Mary to sit patiently on a chair while we lecture to them about God and the other important issues of life. Instead, they are equipped with internal "motors" which are incapable of idling. Their transmissions consist of only six gears: run, jump, climb, crawl, slide, and dive. Boys and girls are simply not wired for quiet conversations about heavy topics.

How, then, do conscientious parents convey their attitudes and values and faith to their children? It is done *subtly*, through the routine interactions of everyday living (see Deut. 6:4-9). We saw this fact illustrated in our own home when Danae was ten years old and Ryan was five. We were riding in the car when we passed a porno theater. I believe the name of the particular movie was "Flesh Gordon," or something equally sensuous. Danae, who was sitting in the front seat, pointed to the theater and said,

"That's a dirty movie, isn't it, Dad?"

I nodded affirmatively.

"Is that what they call an X-rated movie?" she asked.

Again, I indicated that she was correct.

Danae thought for a moment or two, then said, "Dirty movies are really bad, aren't they?"

I said, "Yes, Danae. Dirty movies are very evil."

This entire conversation lasted less than a minute, consisting of three brief questions and three replies. Ryan, who was in the back seat, did not enter into our discussion. In fact, I wondered what he thought about the interchange, and concluded that he probably wasn't listening.

I was wrong. Ryan heard the conversation and apparently continued thinking about it for several days. But amusingly, Ryan did not know what a "dirty movie" was. How would a five-year-old boy learn what goes on in such places, since no one had ever discussed pornography with him? Nevertheless, he had his own idea about the subject. That concept was revealed to me four nights later at the close of the day.

Ryan and I got down on our knees to say his bedtime prayer, and the preschooler spontaneously returned to that conversation earlier in the week.

"Dear Lord," he began in great seriousness, "help me not to go see any dirty movies . . . where everyone is spitting on each other."

For Ryan, the dirtiest thing he could imagine would be a salivary free-for-all. That *would* be dirty, I had to admit.

But I also had to acknowledge how *casually* children assimilate our values and attitudes. You see, I had no way of anticipating that brief conversation in the car. It was not my deliberate intention to convey my views about pornography to my children. How was it that they learned one more dimension of my value system on that morning? It occurred because we happened to be together . . . to be talking to one another. Those kinds of subtle, unplanned interactions account for much of the instruction that passes from one generation to the next. It is a powerful force in shaping young lives, *if! If* parents are occasionally at home with their kids; *if* they have the energy to converse with them; *if* they have anything worthwhile to transmit; *if* they care.

My point is that the breathless American life-style is particularly costly to children. Yet 1.8 million youngsters come home to an empty house after school each day. They are called "latchkey" kids because they wear the keys to their front doors around their necks. Not only are their fathers overcommitted and preoccupied, but now, their mothers are energetically seeking fulfillment in the working world, too. So who is at home with the kids? More commonly, the answer is *nobody*.

Have *you* felt the years slipping by with far too many unfulfilled promises to your children? Have you heard yourself saying,

> Son, we've been talking about the wagon we were going to build one of these Saturdays, and I just want you to know that I haven't forgotten it. But we can't do it this weekend 'cause I have to make an unexpected trip to Indianapolis. However, we will get to it one of these days. I'm not sure if it can be next weekend, but you keep reminding me and we'll eventually work together. And I'm going to take you fishing, too. I love to fish and I know a little stream that is jumping with trout in the spring. But this just happens to be a very busy month for your mom and me, so let's keep planning and before you know it, the time will be here.

Then the days soon become weeks, and the weeks flow into months and years and decades . . . and our kids grow up and leave home. Then we sit in the silence of our family rooms, trying to recall the precious experiences that escaped us there. Ringing in our ears is that haunting phrase, "We'll have a good time . . . then . . ."

Oh, I know I'm stirring a measure of guilt into the pot with these words. But perhaps we need to be confronted with the important issues of life, even if they make us uncomfortable. Furthermore, I feel *obligated* to speak on behalf of the millions of children across this country who are reaching for fathers who aren't there. The names of specific boys and girls come to my mind as I write these words, symbolizing the masses of lonely kids who experience the agony of unmet needs. Let me acquaint you with two or three of those children whose paths I have crossed.

I think first of the mother who approached me after I had spoken some years ago. She had supported her husband through college and medical school, only to have him divorce her in favor of a younger plaything. She stood with tears in her eyes as she described the impact of his departure on her two sons.

"They miss their daddy every day," she said. "They don't understand why he doesn't come to see them. The older boy, especially, wants a father so badly that he reaches for every man who comes into our lives. What can I tell him? How can I meet the boy's needs for a father who will hunt and fish and play football and bowl with him and his brother? It's breaking my heart to see them suffer so much."

I gave this mother a few suggestions and offered my understanding and support. The next morning I spoke for the final time at her church. Following the service, I stood on the platform as a line of people waited to tell me good-bye and extend their greetings. Standing in the line was the mother *with* her two sons.

They greeted me with smiles and I shook the older child's hand. Then something happened which I did not recall until I was on my way back to Los Angeles. The boy did not let go of my hand! He gripped it tightly, preventing me from welcoming others who pressed around. To my regret, I realized later that I had unconsciously grasped his arm with my other hand, pulling myself free from his grip. I sat on the plane, realizing the full implications of that incident. You see, this lad *needed* me. He needed a man who could take the place of his renegade father. And I had failed him, just like all the rest. Now I'm left with the memory of a child who said with his eyes, "Could you be a daddy to me?"!

Another child has found a permanent place in my memory, although I don't even know her name. I was waiting to catch a plane at Los Angeles International Airport, enjoying my favorite activity of "people watching." But I was unprepared for the drama about to unfold. Standing near me was an old man who was obviously waiting for someone who should have been on the plane that arrived minutes before. He examined each face intently as the passengers filed past. I thought he seemed unusually distressed as he waited.

Then I saw the little girl who stood by his side. She must have been seven years old, and she, too, was desperately looking for a certain face in the crowd. I have rarely seen a child more anxious than this cute little girl. She clung to the old man's arm, who I assumed to be her grandfather. Then as the last passengers came by, one by one, the girl began to cry silently. She was not merely disappointed in that moment; her little heart was broken. The grandfather also appeared to be fighting back the tears. In fact, he was too upset to comfort the child, who then buried her face in the sleeve of his worn coat.

"Oh, God!" I prayed silently. "What special agony are they experiencing in this hour? Was it the child's mother who abandoned her on that painful day? Did her daddy promise to come and then change his mind?"

My great impulse was to throw my arms around the little girl and shield her from the awfulness of that hour. I wanted her to pour out her grief in the protection of my embrace, but I feared that my intrusion would be misunderstood. So I watched helplessly. Then the old man and the child stood silently as the passengers departed from two other planes, but the anxiety on their faces had turned to despair. Finally, they walked slowly through the terminal and toward the door. Their only sound was the snuffing of the little girl who fought to control her tears.

Where is this child now? God only knows.

If the reader will bear with me, I must introduce you to one other child whose family experience has become so common in the Western world. I was waiting at Shawnee Mission Hospital for word on my dad's heart condition, after he was stricken in September. There in the waiting room was an *American Girl* magazine which caught my attention. (I must have been desperate for something to read to have been attracted to the *American Girl*.)

I opened the cover page and immediately saw a composition written by a 14-year-old girl named Vicki Kraushaar. She had submitted her story for publication in the section of the magazine entitled "By You." I'll let Vicki introduce herself and describe her experience.

That's the Way Life Goes Sometimes

> When I was ten, my parents got a divorce. Naturally, my father told me about it, because he was my favorite. [Notice that Vicki did not say, "I was *his* favorite."]
>
> "Honey, I know it's been kind of bad for you these past few days, and I don't want to make it worse. But there's something I have to tell you. Honey, your mother and I got a divorce."
>
> "But, Daddy—"
>
> "I know you don't want this, but it has to be done. Your mother and I just don't get along like we used to. I'm already packed and my plane is leaving in half an hour."
>
> "But, Daddy, why do you have to leave?"
>
> "Well, honey, your mother and I can't live together anymore."
>
> "I know that, but I mean why do you have to leave town?"
>
> "Oh. Well, I got someone waiting for me in New Jersey."
>
> "But, Daddy, will I ever see you again?"
>
> "Sure you will, honey. We'll work something out."
>
> "But what? I mean, you'll be living in New Jersey, and I'll be

living here in Washington."

"Maybe your mother will agree to you spending two weeks in the summer and two in the winter with me."

"Why not more often?"

"I don't think she'll agree to two weeks in the summer and two in the winter, much less more."

"Well, it can't hurt to try."

"I know, honey, but we'll have to work it out later. My plane leaves in 20 minutes and I've got to get to the airport. Now I'm going to get my luggage, and I want you to go to your room so you don't have to watch me. And no long good-byes either."

"Okay, Daddy. Good-bye. Don't forget to write."

"I won't. Good-bye. Now go to your room."

"Okay. Daddy, I don't want you to go!"

"I know, honey. But I have to."

"Why?"

"You wouldn't understand, honey."

"Yes, I would."

"No, you wouldn't."

"Oh well. Good-bye."

"Good-bye. Now go to your room. Hurry up."

"Okay. Well, I guess that's the way life goes sometimes."

"Yes honey. That's the way life goes sometimes."

After my father walked out that door, I never heard from him again. (Reprinted by permission from *American Girl*, a magazine for all girls published by Girl Scouts of the U.S.A.)

Vicki speaks eloquently on behalf of a million American children who have heard those shattering words, "Honey, your mother and I are getting a divorce." Throughout the world, husbands and wives are responding to the media blitz which urges and goads them to do their own thing, to chase impulsive desires without regard for the welfare of their families.

"The kids will get over it," goes the rationalization.

Every form of mass communication seemed mobilized to spread the "me first" philosophy during the 1970s and early 1980s. Frank Sinatra said it musically in his song "I did it *my* way." Sammy Davis, Jr., echoed the sentiment in "I've gotta be me." Robert J. Ringer provided the literary version in *Looking*

Out for Number One, which became the best-selling book in America for 46 weeks. It was flanked by *Open Marriage*, *Creative Divorce*, and *Pulling Your Own Strings*, among hundreds of other dangerous best sellers. The est program then sold the same sickness under the guise of psychological health.

It all sounded so noble at the time. It was called "the discovery of personhood," and it offered an intoxicating appeal to our selfish lusts. But when this insidious philosophy had wormed its way into our system of values, it began to rot us from within. First, it encouraged an insignificant flirtation with sin (perhaps with a man or woman from New Jersey) followed by passion and illicit sexual encounters, followed by camouflaging lies and deceit, followed by angry words and sleepless nights, followed by tears and anguish, followed by crumbling self-esteem, followed by attorneys and divorce courts and property settlements, followed by devastating custody hearings. And from deep within the maelstrom, we can hear the cry of three wounded children—two girls and a boy—who will never fully recover. "Then when lust hath conceived, it bringeth forth sin; and sin, when it is finished, bringeth forth death" (James 1:15, KJV).

For those younger fathers whose children are still at an impressionable age, please believe the words of my dad, "The greatest delusion is to suppose that our children will be devout Christians simply because their parents have been, or that *any* of them will enter into the Christian faith in any other way than through their parents' deep travail of prayer and faith."

If you doubt the validity of this assertion, may I suggest that you read the story of Eli in 1 Samuel 2–4. Here is the account of a priest and servant of God who failed to discipline his children. He was apparently too busy with the "work of the church" to be a leader in his own home. The two boys grew up to be evil young men on whom God's judgment fell.

It concerned me to realize that Eli's service to the Lord was insufficient to compensate for his failure at home. Then I read farther in the narrative and received confirmation of the principle. *Samuel,* the saintly man of God, who stood like a tower of spiritual strength throughout his life, grew up in Eli's home. He watched Eli systematically losing his children, yet Samuel proceeded to fail with his family, too! That was a deeply disturbing truth. If God would not honor Samuel's dedication by guaranteeing the salvation of his children, will He do more for *me* if I'm too busy to do my "homework"?

Having been confronted with these spiritual obligations and responsibilities, the Lord then gave me an enormous burden for my two children. I carry it to this day. There are times when it becomes so heavy that I ask God to remove it from my shoulders, although the concern is not motivated by the usual problems or anxieties. Our kids are apparently healthy and seem to be holding their own emotionally and academically. (Update: Danae finished college in 1990 and Ryan was completing his junior year at the time this was written.) The source of my burden derives from the awareness that a "tug of war" is being waged for the hearts and minds of every person on earth, including these two precious human beings. Satan would deceive and destroy them if given the opportunity, and they will soon have to choose the path they will take.

This mission of introducing one's children to the Christian faith can be likened to a three-man relay race. First, your father runs his lap around the track, carrying the baton, which represents the gospel of Jesus Christ. At the appropriate moment, he hands the baton to you, and you begin your journey around the track. Then finally, the time will come when you must get the baton safely in the hands of your child. But as any track coach will testify, *relay races are won or lost in the transfer of the baton.* There is a critical moment when all can be lost by a fumble or miscalculation. The baton is rarely dropped on the back side of the track when the runner has it firmly in his grasp. If failure is to occur, it will likely happen in the exchange between generations!

According to the Christian values which govern my life, my most important reason for living is to get the baton—the gospel—safely in the hands of my children. Of course, I want to place it in as many other hands as possible, and I'm deeply devoted to the ministry to families that God has given me. *Nevertheless, my number one responsibility is to evangelize my own children.* In the words of my dad, everything else appears "pale and washed out" when compared with that fervent desire. There is no higher calling on the face of the earth.

(Taken from *Straight Talk: What Men Need to Know, What Women Should Understand,* by Dr. James C. Dobson [Dallas: Word, 1991], pp. 59-60, 63-66, 68-73, 77-79, 82.)

A Man and His Family
Personal Evaluation

On a scale from 1 to 10, rate yourself in the following areas, with 1 being "terrible" and 10 being "perfect." If you're comfortable with the idea and really want to gain some additional insight, you might also have your wife or kids rate you in these areas. If you aren't married but have children, skip to question 6. If you're single and not a father, answer the following question: What can I do now to prepare to be a good husband and father if God leads me into marriage?

1. My wife and I have a clearly defined menu of expectations regarding our relationship and our family. _____
2. My wife and I understand and regularly engage in meaningful communication. ______
3. My wife and I are involved in a small support group to help us strengthen our marriage and family. _____
4. My wife and I recognize our personal and emotional wounds suffered in the past, and we have learned how to compensate for them. _____
5. My wife and I are dependent on the Lord Jesus Christ for quality life.
6. I spend plenty of quality time with each of my children._____ (How many minutes a day would you estimate you spend talking with each child?______)
7. My children know my values, and they are picking up the values and attitudes I care deeply about. _____
8. When I make a promise to my children, they know I will always keep it.______
9. When it comes to the ultimate purpose in life, each of my children understands how I feel about a relationship with Jesus Christ and shares that core value with me._____

Now review your list. Does one area stand out as something that needs the most attention right now? What will you work on first? In that number-one area, what one thing could you do to help move that rating closer to 10? (You might ask for help here from your wife or children.)

In the Group

1. Talk about how you did this past week in the activity you selected to help move you closer to purity.
2. In 60 seconds or less, describe the quality of marriage you saw in your parents' relationship as a child. (Each member should do this.)
3. Complete the following statement: I would describe the quality of time my father spent with me when I was a boy as . . .
(Each member should do this.)
4. Do the answers to questions 2 and 3 give you any insights into the success or failure of your own marriage and parenting? For singles—do these answers give you insight into your potential for success in your future family (if you have one)?

Next, based on the needs of your group, you can focus the remaining discussion on either marriage or fathering.

Marriage

5. What are some of the things on your menu of expectations for your relationship with your wife (or if you're single, with your future mate)?
6. How meaningful is communication with your wife? What can you do in the next week to make it more meaningful *for her?*

Fathering

5. How do you express your values to your children (by telling them, by what you do, by how you spend your time and money, by what you read or watch on TV, etc.)?
6. Have you heard someone say recently, or have you said: "Well, I'm not spending much time with my children, but it's not really the quantity of time that's so important, it's the quality of time"? What is your feeling about that statement?
7. What changes can you make now in order to spend more time with your children? How?

Memory Verse: "Husbands, love your wives, just as Christ loved the church and gave himself up for her. . . . Fathers, do not exasperate your children; instead, bring them up in the training and instruction of the Lord" (Eph. 5:25; 6:4).

On Your Own

1. Write down one activity you plan to do this week to strengthen your marriage or parenting. Write it in your Day-Timer or on a 3x5 card to remind yourself.
2. Read Promise 5, "A Man and His Church," prior to the next meeting.

Promise 5

A Man and His Church

A Promise Keeper is committed to supporting the mission of his church by honoring and praying for his pastor, and by actively giving his time and resources.

PROMISE 5

Introduction

We've worked through four promises so far. Each has focused on some vital part of our relationship with God, our families, or a few key friends. Starting with this promise, we begin to expand our perspective. A Promise Keeper doesn't live in isolation. He is part of a larger community. We will look at three aspects of that: a man's commitment to his church, to his brothers in Christ in other denominations and across racial and ethnic lines, and to the world as we live out Christ's Great Commandment and Great Commission.

We begin in this section with the church. First, we look at two things you can do for your own pastor that will encourage and energize him in his ministry. They aren't hard, nor are they time consuming, but they are vital to his well-being. And anyone can do them. Pastor Dale Schlafer, in a moving chapter, shows us this secret. Dale is senior pastor at South Evangelical Presbyterian Fellowship of Littleton, Colorado. He is also chairman of the board for Promise Keepers.

Then a man who has pastored for more than 30 years tells about some of the men who made a difference in his churches. You'll see that in many cases, what they did wasn't extraordinary. Rather, they were faithful to be who God had made them to be. H.B. London, Jr., is the author of this chapter and is vice president in charge of pastoral ministries for Focus on the Family. Prior to that, he was pastor of Nazarene churches in California and Oregon.

Honoring and Praying for Your Pastor

by
Dale Schlafer

I was in Cincinnati for a conference in which I was playing a significant role, and I was afraid. I had been given a large responsibility, and I questioned my ability to handle it. I had told my church these feelings on the Sunday prior to my two-week absence. I had pleaded with them for prayer. Now, nine days later, I returned to my hotel and stopped off at the front desk to see if I had received any mail. I had a telegram, the clerk said; it contained only three words: "We Love You!"

That message was followed by 12 pages of single-spaced, typed names of people from my church. During the announcements at church the day before, the congregation had been reminded that the upcoming Tuesday was my big day. Anyone who wanted to encourage me was invited to stop in the back and sign up for the telegram. As I read those names, all 12 pages, I felt ten feet tall. I knew they were praying and thinking about me. At that moment, I felt I could have done anything because I was so affirmed and supported.

That evening, one of my best friends (also a pastor) and I went to see the Cincinnati Reds play a baseball game. While we were sitting in the stands, I told him about the telegram. Even years later, as I sit writing this, I can still see his face. He looked me straight in the eyes and, with tears running down his cheeks, said, "Once, just once, I wish somebody in my church would tell me they loved me."

What I have discovered since that night, and what surveys of pastors show, is that an overwhelming number of ministers share my friend's sentiment. They feel unloved, unappreciated, and unprayed for.

Promise Keepers is committed to changing this situation by calling men to "honor and pray for their pastors."

Honor

All Christians are called to practice honor. Romans 12:10 says, "Honor one another above yourselves." God calls us to esteem, respect, and show deference to each other in the Body of Christ. When it comes to pastors, however, the Word of God says something unique. We read in 1 Thessalonians 5:12-13, "Now we ask you, brothers, to respect those who work hard among you, who are over you in the Lord and who admonish you. Hold them in the highest regard in love because of their work."

The phrase "Hold them in the highest regard" is unusual in the original Greek of the New Testament in that it takes the adverb and triples its intensity. This verse could read, "Hold them beyond the highest regard in love." Or it might be rendered, "Honor, honor, honor in love those who work hard among you." In today's wording, we might paraphrase it, "Esteem to the max in love those who work hard among you." What we sense here is the apostle Paul's struggle—almost being at a loss for words—to adequately express what the Holy Spirit wants to communicate to the church, just how much the people in a congregation are to hold their pastor in super highest regard. Pastors are not to be esteemed for their office, degrees, age, or spiritual gifts, but "because of their work."

The biblical pattern, then, is for all Christians to show honor to one another, and triple honor to their pastors.

Now, if that's the case, why are pastors not honored in our day? First, our culture encourages us to not show honor to anyone. We live in a day of egalitarianism that doesn't allow for differences and appears to treat all people the same. Political and sports cartoonists ridicule those in authority. Comedians poke fun at anyone in a place of prominence. And the average Christian carries that same attitude into the church.

I believe the major reason pastors are not honored, however, is that church members don't know it's one of their responsibilities in following Jesus Christ. Some church members simply enjoy tearing down their pastor, but the vast majority fail to honor their pastor just because they are ignorant of God's

Word. One pastor, Steve, with whom I spoke in preparation for writing this chapter brought some men from his church to the Promise Keepers '93 conference. He told me that since then, things had changed dramatically because his men heard Coach McCartney talk about a man's responsibility to his pastor. "The men of my church didn't have bad hearts," Steve said. "They just needed an external source to explain the truth of God's Word to them."

How is it that people in the church don't know this teaching to honor their pastors? The answer is that it hasn't been taught. I searched through the books of sermons in my library, some many years old and others quite contemporary, but I could not find one sermon on this topic. Given our age, it's obvious why this is the case. Can you imagine your pastor standing in the pulpit next Sunday and stating, no matter how smoothly, "You as a church body are to give me triple honor"? As soon as you entered your car, you would be saying, "What an egotist! I can't believe the turkey would say something like that. Wow, is he ever full of pride!" Because that's the way most people would react, pastors shy away from this teaching, and the American church continues in its ignorant disobedience to this clear command of God.

Promise Keepers is committed to seeing that this biblical truth is recaptured in the church. By the grace of God, we are determined to eliminate the neglect and dishonor of our pastors. With fierce determination, Christian men are being called to take the lead in bringing triple honor to our pastors.

What would it look like to honor our pastors? Let's take a closer look at Steve's story.

In his own words, Steve was "at a point of depression." Disheartened with the ministry at his church, he had already written a letter of resignation. In fact, the letter was signed and on his desk when he and some of his men left for the Promise Keepers conference. As the men listened to Coach Mac, they came under strong conviction for their failure to honor their pastor. And during a sharing time in the worship service the next Sunday, a number of them stood and repented of their sin of not honoring and encouraging their pastor. They also acknowledged their sin of expecting him to do all the ministry while they stood on the sidelines and griped.

"Overnight there was a change in my church," Steve said. "The entire dynamic of our church is changing. They have freed me to do what I was called to do. Beyond that, they have started a Monday morning prayer time where a part of the time is devoted to prayer for me." With great delight,

Steve ripped up his letter of resignation, and he and his church are now working together as a team. Why? Part of the answer has to be that the men came to see the biblical necessity of honoring their pastor. As a result of their obedience, God is now free to pour out His blessing.

Perhaps you're thinking at this point, *Could this honoring thing go too far? Could this feed an ego problem? Might this cause jealousy?* Undoubtedly, those concerns are possibilities. If I were writing to pastors, I would digress at this point to deal with the sins of pride and arrogance with which pastors might be tempted. But right now, at this point in the history of the American church, those sins are not the problem. The hurt, the neglect, the dishonoring have gone on for so long, and with such intensity, that large numbers of pastors are turning in their resignations because they feel so alone and unsupported. One recent poll revealed that 80 percent of the pastors responding had thought about quitting in the last three months. Yes, in some immature men, triple honoring might cause a problem. But for the vast majority of godly pastors, honoring and lifting them up will cause them to be more motivated and even harder workers. They will be encouraged, and their churches will be blessed.

As a pastor, I, too, stood on the floor of the football stadium at Promise Keepers '93. I reveled in the prolonged standing ovation the more than 50,000 gathered men gave to all the pastors who were there. In the providence of God, I stood next to a pastor I didn't know. He said, "This will be enough for me to be able to put up with all the ——— I'll take at my church for the next six months!" Honoring him in this manner had put a new resolve and a new desire in his heart to go back and pastor his church in what was obviously a tough situation. Now, if the men of that church honored and encouraged him regularly, what effect would it have?

What would happen if you regularly honored and encouraged your pastor? I believe your church would begin to receive blessing as never before. Why? Because the blessing of God comes when we obey His Word.

Prayer

Promise Keepers are also committed to praying for their pastors. The concept of praying for all Christians is clearly spelled out in the Bible: "And pray in the Spirit on all occasions with all kinds of prayers and requests. With this in mind, be alert and always keep on praying for all the saints" (Eph. 6:18).

When it comes to praying for our pastors, we have a special responsibility.

Paul, an apostle and pastor, said, "I urge you, brothers, by our Lord Jesus Christ and by the love of the Spirit, to join me in my struggle by praying to God for me" (Rom. 15:30). In another place, he reminded his readers that they could help him and his ministry team "by your prayers" (2 Cor. 1:11). In other words, pastors especially are in need of prayer.

Why is that the case? Satan's desire is to destroy the work of Christ in the world. One of his most effective ways of doing that is to destroy pastors. If Satan can bring them down, causing disgrace and ridicule to taint the work of Christ, the nonbelieving world will not be attracted to Jesus. We have all seen the carnage left around us as pastors have failed morally or have simply left the ministry because of disillusionment.

Several years ago, a pastor in Denver told his congregation the following true story. A lady from his church was flying back to Denver, and as the meal was served, she noticed the woman sitting next to her did not take a meal. To make conversation, the Christian woman asked, "Are you on a diet?"

"No," came the reply, "I am a member of the church of Satan, and we are fasting for the destruction of the families of pastors and Christian leaders."

Pastors are at risk because they are the church's leaders. If Satan can get them, the church of Jesus Christ will be crippled.

In no way am I trying to excuse the pastors who have fallen or bailed out of the ministry in recent years, but I do have a question. How many of those pastors had men in their churches who daily brought them before the Lord in prayer? I wonder how many men's groups gathered to pray for them? I am not surprised by the number of pastors who have fallen. To be truthful, I'm surprised the number is not larger. The job of being a pastor is enormously difficult and is made even more so because the men of the church are not praying.

Pastors need prayer especially for their preaching and teaching of the Word. Again I ask, why are pastors not preaching what they really believe is the word of God for their congregations? The answer is, I believe, that they are afraid—afraid the people of their churches will not accept the kind of preaching that clearly and powerfully confronts sin and sinners. Afraid they will be fired and lose their financial security. As a result, in many cases, God's purposes are thwarted and our churches remain weak and sick.

The apostle Paul regularly asked for prayer so that "boldness might be given." Pastors need to know their men are with them and are praying for them so they can be emboldened to share the whole council of God and not cower in the face of opposition within or without the church.

E.M. Bounds said it this way:

> The men in the pew given to praying for the pastor are like poles which hold up the wires along which the electric current runs. They are not the power, neither are they the specific agents in making the Word of the Lord effective. But they hold up the wires upon which the divine power runs to the hearts of men. . . . They make conditions favorable for the preaching of the Gospel. (*A Treasury of Prayer—The Best of E. M. Bounds* [Minneapolis: Bethany House, 1961], pp. 172-73)

I don't understand it all; I just know that when the men of the church start praying for the pastor, something happens.

Dr. Wilbur Chapman often told of going to Philadelphia to become the pastor of the Wanamaker Church. After his first sermon, an older gentleman met him in front of the pulpit and said, "You are pretty young to be the pastor of this great church. We have always had older pastors. I am afraid you won't succeed. But you preach the gospel, and I am going to help you all I can."

"I looked at him," said Dr. Chapman, "and said to myself: 'Here's a crank.' But the old gentleman continued: 'I am going to pray for you that you may have the Holy Spirit's power upon you, and two others have covenanted to join me.' " Then Dr. Chapman related the outcome:

> I did not feel so bad when I learned he was going to pray for me. The three became ten, the ten became twenty, the twenty became fifty, the fifty became two hundred who met before the service to pray that the Holy Spirit might come upon me. In another room, eighteen elders knelt so close around me to pray for me that I could put out my hands and touch them on all sides. I always went into the pulpit feeling that I would have the anointing in answer to the prayers of two hundred and nineteen men. It was easy to preach, a very joy. Anybody could preach with such conditions. And what was the result? We received 1,100 into our church by conversion in three years, 600 of which were men. I do not see how the average preacher under average conditions preaches at all. Church members have much more to do than go to church as curious, idle spectators, to be amused and entertained. It is their business to pray mightily that the Holy

Ghost will clothe the preacher and make his words like dynamite.

(John Maxwell, in a letter to church leaders, quoting A.M. Hills in *Pentecostal Light*)

Imagine what would happen if you and the other men from your church determined to pray for your pastor. The whole dynamic and atmosphere of your church would be different.

What would it look like to start such a prayer ministry? In the church I serve, men are asked once a year to sign up to be prayer partners with me. At least one man is assigned to pray for me each day of the month. When that list is drawn up, I pray for the man who is praying for me on that day as well. To further assist my prayer partners, I regularly send them a letter to keep them current on answers to their prayers and new things for which they can be praying.

The entire group that signed up is also divided into four teams. Each team is assigned one Sunday a month to come to the church to pray for me. (Fifth Sundays are left unassigned, and any team member can come. Usually, the meetings are packed!) The men arrive at 8:15 A.M., as our first service is at 9:00. They disperse throughout the entire church facility. Some stay in the worship center, praying for the worship team and others participating in the service, as well as for those who will attend the services. Others move through the classrooms, praying for teachers by name. Still others walk in the parking lot, asking God to keep things organized and friendly, and that the sweet Spirit of Jesus will be sensed by folks as they pull into the lot. At 8:30, we all gather in my office, and they pray for me. I tell them what I think God wants me to do that day, plus how I am feeling both physically and spiritually. Then I kneel and the men gather around, lay hands on me, and begin to pray.

The results have been dramatic. I have sensed a new power and authority in my preaching. The men who pray have a sense of personal ownership of Sunday mornings. They know their prayers are essential if anything of eternal significance is to take place. Further, the Lord has built a wonderful sense of teamwork through this prayer partnership. Sometimes as I'm preaching, I catch the eye of one of them, and he'll wink or give me the thumbs-up sign. When that occurs, I know they are praying and are *for* me, and then I really "go to preachin'!"

Let me suggest that you go to your pastor and tell him you want to organize a team of men who will pray for him every day. Tell him you and this group of men wish to meet with him on Sundays before services to pray for the anointing of the Holy Spirit to come upon him. If you do this, it will be one of the greatest joys your pastor has ever had in his ministry.

Why do I know that's true? Because the overwhelming majority of pastors feel unprayed for and isolated in their ministries. One pastor said to me not long ago, "Nobody in my church cares about me or the ministry of this church." Suppose the men of his church came around him and asked to pray for him. What do you think would happen? That church would never be the same again.

Conclusion

Promise Keepers is seeking nothing less than a paradigm shift in the life of our churches. Until now, in the vast majority of situations, pastors have not been honored, loved, esteemed, or prayed for. By God's grace, however, that is going to change as Promise Keepers in every church see it as their personal responsibility to support the pastor. That's why I say we want a paradigm shift. A *paradigm* is a model, or pattern, for understanding and interpreting reality.

When there's a paradigm shift, everything gets changed. As Promise Keepers begin to honor and pray for their pastors, a new life and vitality will start to grow in congregations. A new teamwork will blossom between pastor and people. A new sense of call will dominate the pastors of this land. A new holiness will spring forth because of changed preaching. And we will find ourselves in the middle of revival.

At Promise Keepers '93, Coach McCartney said the following:

> I see us going home to our churches and asking our pastors for permission, praying fervently for the favor of God, to stand before the congregation and say: "Things are going to change around here. We're going to start to lift up our pastor. We are going to start to stand in the gap for our preacher. We're going to pray around the clock! We're going to build this man up. We're going to take him where he has never been before." I see us exploding in our churches.

Indeed! That is our goal—to see revival spread across our country. How will that occur? Revival will come as churches are revived. The churches will be revived as the pastors are revived. And part of what God will use to revive them will be Promise Keepers, men who keep their word to honor and pray for their pastors.

The Man God Seeks

by
H.B. London, Jr.

My interest in the role men play in the life of the church was ignited in my first pastorate. It was a small church in a lower-income section of Southern California. The church was mainly made up of women who either dominated the home or attended the church alone because their husbands were unsaved. It had been, and continues to be, an unhealthy church; when men do not take the leadership in a church, it will never be balanced. It will remain a vulnerable organization that has no noticeable impact on its community.

> William Bennett put it succinctly in a 1986 speech on the family in Chicago when he asked, "Where are the fathers? . . . Generally, the mothers are there struggling. For nine out of ten children in single parent homes, the father is the one who isn't there. One-fifth of all American children live in homes without fathers. . . . Where are the fathers? Where are the men?" (James Dobson and Gary L. Bauer, *Children at Risk* [Dallas: Word, 1990], p. 167)

That little church had no self-esteem. And though we experienced three years of growth, it was not a foundational growth. It was growth that emerged out of crises and my efforts. I learned a major lesson there. I really don't mean for this statement to sound chauvinistic, but I learned that I should never again pastor a church that didn't have strong male leadership. Except I did.

My second church was in a steel-mill town. The mill worked three shifts, and, you guessed it, the women made most of the decisions in our fellowship. I learned how to work with the ladies "of influence," but I couldn't help but notice the effect that had on every facet of the church. In every major decision, the men would grow quiet as the ladies had the final say. This pattern not only hurt the church, but it was also evident in their home and business lives. The way children were raised, where vacations were taken—all those things were met with a sense of disinterest on the part of the men.

I've seen the same pattern in other churches as well. And I've seen men seek their acceptance in other ways and from other people.

Do I blame the women? Not at all. They were taking places they had been given. If men forfeit leadership in the church, they disregard the command of God. If they grow silent when it comes to making major decisions, they have no one to blame but themselves. If a man abdicates his responsibility in the home as the head of the house and shuffles the role of discipline off to the mother—in most cases, the consequences will be painful.

Lessons Learned

After seven years of fairly successful ministry, I accepted an assignment to a church in the Northwest. I was still a young minister, but I had learned a great deal. I was determined I would put a greater emphasis on winning men to Jesus Christ and urging them to take up the mantle of leadership. It was more than just a dream; it was a matter of economics. I had learned that in more than 90 percent of those homes where the man took leadership or came to know Christ, the whole family would follow. The wife would be relieved of her burden to fashion the spiritual life of her family, and the children would gladly follow their dad's lead. In many ways, it gave the whole family a focus—something in common, something to do together.

That emphasis worked. The church, over a period of years, became one of the largest in the denomination I served. Because of the men? No! Because we had a balance of leadership in the church. It was the way God intended the church to operate. Now we had the best of both worlds—male and female leaders sharing the burden for their families and their community. Every church must have that equality of leadership. How can it be achieved? Let me explain.

My church in the Northwest had a strong male presence, but it was not a sensitive presence. It was more bottom-line oriented than it was ministry minded. We didn't see a lot of love, but we did see a lot of pride. I worked hard to change that pattern. I gave my life to those men, investing great amounts of time and energy with them while never neglecting the needs of their wives and families. I developed a breakfast, lunch, and athletic outreach.

Nearly every day of the work week, I would spend up to four hours with men. Some days I would have two breakfasts or two lunches, or we would meet in their offices or work places. In those meetings, I would do three things, all of them centered on a kind of personal interaction.

The first thing I did was to try to discover what kind of spiritual background the man had. Only a low percentage of people in the Northwest attend church. It wasn't unusual to find men who had absolutely no church or religious influence. I asked questions such as, "Did you attend Sunday school as a kid?" "Did your folks go with you to church?" "Did you have a favorite pastor?" "Did many of your friends in high school attend church?" Such questions would often lead to more discussions about my guests' backgrounds. Often I would uncover a great deal of disillusionment about the church—distrust, even contempt. But at least it gave me an opening. I was never judgmental or condemning. Instead, I was sympathetic. A lot of men have lived under condemnation from family, friends, and church leaders for so long that they feel they can never measure up.

My second goal was to establish a common ground for further dialogue. In a simple manner, I would get the man talking about himself. Most guys are not given to a lot of conversation, but if you find a point of interest, they will talk. Many like to discuss sports and work. They come alive when they can remember interesting events in their lives. I would just sit back and let it flow. I learned so much from men who had both won and lost in life, love, and relationships. I also learned that men seldom have the stage to themselves—in a setting where they don't have to compete with a television program, kids, wives, or other guys. And I learned that our lunch or breakfast setting was not a time for me to try to impress my guests. It was their spotlight. I made no attempt to upstage them; I was all ears. What a valuable experience that was! It helped me learn more about the pressures, temptations, and fears my men were facing.

I also spent a lot of time on their turf—basketball courts, baseball diamonds, golf courses, athletic events, and even in their workplaces. All of these became forums for evangelism and friendship. The fact that someone really cared was the obvious attraction. I purposely tried to come out from behind my "clergy cloak" and be real. For some, I became a father figure; for others, a brother they never had; for most, a friend they could trust. They all needed me to show an honest interest in their lives.

The final gesture of interest I tried to offer was follow-up. I didn't just cut and run. I wanted the men to know I wasn't seeking another notch on my church-growth belt, but I cared for them because they were important to me. How did I convey my concern? By a simple phrase like "If you ever need me, just call." "Is there a way I can pray for you?" "I'll talk to you soon." Most importantly, I meant what I said.

When I was a young minister, a United States senator took an interest in me and made me feel special. I will never forget the time I made a trip to Washington, D. C. I was frightened at the thought of walking into the Senate office building. But the senator greeted me warmly—as if I were somebody important—and took me for lunch in the Senate dining room, where I had some of its famous bean soup. After lunch, the senator walked me through the nation's capitol, stopping to point out things of interest. Then we walked into a little room like a miniature chapel located off the Capitol rotunda. There we knelt at a small altar, and he prayed for me. For me! As I was leaving, the senator said, "Pastor, if you ever need me, please feel free to call."

I shall never forget that time. And from it I learned that no one is unworthy. Everyone counts. God loves each of us as though we were the only one to love.

That phrase—"If you ever need me, please feel free to call"—became a part of my ministry to men. They did call—they still do.

I learned a lot from dedicated men about how to pastor them. They helped me minister to their real needs, not those I had imagined. For instance, one day a prominent surgeon walked into my office. I was new to the church. He was highly respected both in the community and in our congregation. To be honest, I was intimidated by him. We made small talk for a while, and then he left. I wondered why he had come to see me; he never really said.

In a few minutes, my office phone rang. It was the doctor, and he said, "H.B., I really needed you today, but you didn't seem to notice. Can you imagine walking into my office—sitting on the examination table—and me not asking you what your needs were?"

My response was a feeble, "No."

He went on. "I needed you to pray with me today. I was experiencing some traumatic family difficulties. You failed me today. But pastor, I am going to give you another chance."

When he hung up, I dropped my head and thanked God for the lesson He had just taught me—painful but worthwhile. I became acutely aware of my responsibility to those God allowed across my path. I was honored to pray for men. And when it was proper, I prayed for them regardless of the surroundings.

I have often been asked why I would make such a time-consuming, often-disappointing investment in men. My response: It is God's plan for His church. I was seeking, with His help, to develop a breed of Christian men who would live up to the expectations of 2 Timothy 2:2: "And the things you have heard me say in the presence of many witnesses entrust to reliable men who will also be qualified to teach others."

The Man God Wants

Let me describe the kind of man I believe God seeks in this complex world. And let me begin by asking how you see yourself. What would folks say of you as they looked at your relationship to God and the church? My hope and prayer is that you would measure up to some men in the Bible who were described in a few words:

Abraham was faithful and believed in God (see Heb. 11:8-12; Gen. 15:6).
Barnabas was a "Son of Encouragement" (Acts 4:36).
David was "a man after [God's] own heart" (1 Sam. 13:14).
Hezekiah "did what was right in the eyes of the LORD" (2 Kings 18:3).
Job "was blameless and upright; he feared God and shunned evil" (Job 1:1).
Noah "was a righteous man, blameless among the people of his time, and he walked with God" (Gen. 6:9).
Moses "was a very humble man" (Num. 12:3).
Demetrius "is well spoken of by everyone—and even by the truth itself" (3 John 12).
Solomon received from God "wisdom and very great insight, and a breadth of understanding as measureless as the sand on the seashore" (1 Kings 4:29).
Timothy "is faithful in the Lord" (1 Cor. 4:17).
Enoch "walked with God" (Gen. 5:24).
Stephen was "a man full of God's grace and power" (Acts 6:8).
Simeon "was righteous and devout" (Luke 2:25).
Jesus was "full of joy through the Holy Spirit" (Luke 10:21).
Cornelius (the centurion) "and all his family were devout and God-fearing" (Acts 10:2).

Jonathan "became one in spirit with David, and he loved him as himself" (1 Sam. 18:1).

I'm sure you get the picture.

I am moved by the one who wrote, "Since we are surrounded by such a great cloud of witnesses, let us throw off everything that hinders and the sin that so easily entangles, and let us run with perseverance the race marked out for us. Let us fix our eyes on Jesus, the author and perfecter of our faith, who for the joy set before him endured the cross, scorning its shame, and sat down at the right hand of the throne of God" (Heb. 12:1-2).

Our lives in Christ are identifiable. People can see what our values are—how we face a crisis; the way we treat our families; how we relate to the awesome commands of God; and where our priorities are placed. So what would others say of you? "He is: Faithful! Moral! Full of integrity! Prayerful! Humble! Obedient! Devout! Committed to his family!" Or maybe a combination of those things. Regardless, you have identifying characteristics.

From my 30 years of ministry, a handful of men really stand out in my mind. I would do them an injustice to call them by their real names, but I hope they will recognize themselves.

Howard: Willing to involve himself in thankless, menial chores. He was invaluable. He was a true servant.

Gerald: The most generous person I have ever known. He really believed that all he possessed belonged to God. He was a caretaker. He was also greatly blessed.

Alan: An encourager. He stood by his pastor in a way that was commendable. He also wrote notes, made phone calls, and did things for the leaders of his church that were not expected. He was selfless but had a healthy view of himself.

Ralph: He prayed. I mean he *prayed.* Sometimes he would even embarrass me because he prayed so much and in unlikely places. But whenever I needed someone to pray for me, you can be assured, I called on him. I still do.

James: He was totally devoted to Jesus Christ and found great pleasure in doing His will. He placed a high priority on church attendance and using his gifts to God's honor. He did not flaunt his faith. He simply lived it, and people could see in him a difference that often demanded an explanation.

Carl: He really loved his family. It was natural, not something contrived. He went about his duties as husband and father in a way that caused some of us to stand in awe. Next to his love for the Lord, his family took priority over everything else.

Martin: The model of integrity. He lived behind closed doors as openly and honestly as if he were being observed by the church leadership. You could trust him with a confidence. He refused to be caught up in gossip or idle chatter. He was a man without guile, but he didn't parade his integrity. He just lived it.

John: He was a friend. He didn't need you to nurse the friendship. He was loyal. Honest with you. He held you accountable without being judgmental. He was not perfect, but he was consistently good and available to talk and listen.

Bill: What a student! At times he was obsessed with a thirst for knowledge. The Bible was truly a "light and lamp" for him; it gave clarity to his living. He was very teachable, too.

Lou: He was steadfast. His life was full of pain and disappointment, but he never worried. Like Job and Paul, he realized he was a sojourner on this earth; he was not to pitch a tent here but to live expectantly. Sorrow was for a little while. He was more than a conqueror. He didn't fight life; he lived it, and he made us all feel like winners.

At this point, as I think back over the men I've known and pastored, I feel like the writer of Hebrews when he said,

> And what more shall I say? I do not have time
> to tell about Gideon, Barak, Samson, Jephthah, David,
> Samuel and the prophets, who through faith
> conquered kingdoms, administered justice, and gained
> what was promised; who shut the mouths of lions,
> quenched the fury of the flames, and escaped the
> edge of the sword; whose weakness was turned to
> strength; and who became powerful in battle and routed
> foreign armies. (Heb. 11:32-34)

I don't mean to bore you with a run-through of people I've been honored to pastor. Their lives, however, were not only beneficial to the church, but also to me personally. I was called to a new plateau of holy living because of them. I am grateful to God for allowing them into my life.

As I look over the list of names, however, I realize none of those men was perfect. They all had flaws and rough edges. They all needed improvement. But they recognized and continued to work on their weak points. I believe that is the real mark of maturity. When we see a need in our lives, we do not walk away from it; we seek God's guidance for healing and correction.

> Do not merely listen to the word, and so deceive yourselves. Do what it says. Anyone who listens to the word but does not do what it says is like a man who looks at his face in a mirror and, after looking at himself, goes away and immediately forgets what he looks like. But the man who looks intently into the perfect law that gives freedom, and continues to do this, not forgetting what he has heard, but doing it—he will be blessed in what he does. (James 1:22-25)

Let me ask: Are you involved in building up the church of Jesus Christ? Do you know your spiritual gifts and use them to strengthen the Body? Those gifts need not be exceptional, but you will shortchange your life in the Body if you don't use what God has given you (see Rom. 12:5-8). We must match our gifts to God's assignments. It will work every time.

For a checklist for the modern churchman, see the personal evaluation at the end of this section.

Our Motivation

T.S. Eliot once said, "The greatest treason is to do the right thing for the wrong reason." Why would we even try to live by a standard that is so totally different from the world's? It would be so easy to do it their way. The answer is simply stated but by no means simply lived out: our love for God and His creation.

The Bible states in 1 Samuel 16:7, "The LORD does not look at the things man looks at. Man looks at the outward appearance, but the LORD looks at the heart."

What we believe is important, but it doesn't stop there. How we act is also a test, the true demonstration of our priorities and convictions. Watch how a man acts and you can, in many ways, determine the level of his commitment to the Lord. Jesus even talked about some who responded positively to

God's voice but then acted out their own wills. In the parable of the two sons, He told of one who, when commanded to work in the vineyard, responded, " 'I will, sir,' but he did not go" (Matt. 21:30). As I see it, the real test is not necessarily creed or conduct, but one's motivation—not what one does, but why one does it. God is interested in motivation. To the teacher of the law He said, " 'Love the Lord your God with all your heart and with all your soul and with all your strength and with all your mind'; and, 'Love your neighbor as yourself' " (Luke 10:27).

And beyond the motivation is the cost. Why would anyone want to pay so high a price for such a life-style? That is a decision every man must make. Will we—do we—really want to serve Christ enough to pay the price He asks? Everyone should consider that cost. Jesus said to His followers, "If anyone would come after me, he must deny himself and take up his cross daily and follow me. For whoever wants to save his life will lose it, but whoever loses his life for me will save it" (Luke 9:23-24).

As you can see, it's not a simple challenge, and it doesn't get any easier when He demands our unquestioned loyalty. Jesus said, "If anyone comes to me and does not hate his father and mother, his wife and children, his brothers and sisters— yes, even his own life—he cannot be my disciple. And anyone who does not carry his cross and follow me cannot be my disciple" (Luke 14:26-27).

It's not an easy decision, but it is a right decision. The men I know who serve, love, and seek Christ best want to do His will above all else.

The badge of Christian discipleship is not a lapel pin, a cross around one's neck, a bumper sticker, or even membership in a church. It's a life-style—an identification with Jesus' words, life, and mission. It is a commitment not just to a cause and a creed, but also to a cross-bearing life-style that demands our very souls.

There is an urgent call in this day for a once-and-for-all loyalty to the mission of Christ, a never-say-die commitment to His person and message. Because we live in a time of fickle followers, fair-weather worshipers, and slumbering saints, it is vital that we take every opportunity to proclaim that it's not easy to be a Christian—it never has been and never will be. Because of that, we need a renewed commitment on the part of those who call Jesus Lord to stand up and be counted regardless of the cost.

As a young minister, I was handed a devotional book by the former chaplain to the United States Senate, Dr. Richard Halverson. One day I ran across something he wrote in that book, *A Day at a Time*, titled "Destination Sickness" (Zondervan, 1974):

> —the syndrome of the man who has arrived and discovered he is nowhere. He has achieved his goals and finds they are not what he had anticipated. He suffers the disillusionment of promises that petered out—the payoff with the kickback! He has all the things money can buy and finds decreasing satisfaction in all he has. He is satiated and unsatisfied. He's got a pot full of nothing. He's in the land of ulcers and cardiacs, alcoholism, divorce and suicide! He suffers from the "neurosis of emptiness." He's the man who has become a whale of a success downtown and a pathetic failure at home. He's a big shot with the boys in the office and a big phony with the boys at home. He's a status symbol in society and a fake with the family. "Destination sickness"—the illness peculiar to a culture that is affluent—and godless.

What's the answer? The cure for all this is Jesus Christ. He is available any time, anywhere, to any man.

You—through Jesus Christ—are the cure. You are the answer to the plight that surrounds our homes and churches. "Blessed are those who hunger and thirst for righteousness" (Matt. 5:6). That's you, my friend. Please don't let us down. No—please don't let down our gracious heavenly Father. You matter a lot!

A Man and His Church
Personal Evaluation

Rate yourself on the following two items on a scale from 1 to 10, with 1 being "terrible" and 10 being "perfect":

1. I and other men in my church regularly honor our pastor. ______
2. I pray daily for my pastor. ______

The following checklist by H.B. London will help you evaluate your church involvement. Answer each question by checking either "Always," "Sometimes," or "Never."

Always	Sometimes	Never	
_____	_____	_____	• Do you belong to a Bible-believing, Bible-teaching church?
_____	_____	_____	• Do you attend church regularly?
_____	_____	_____	• Do you use your spiritual gifts for the building up of the body?
_____	_____	_____	• Do you tithe your income (10%)?
_____	_____	_____	• Do you evangelize and encourage others to attend church and accept Jesus Christ as Lord?
_____	_____	_____	• Do you consider yourself an encourager of the pastor?
_____	_____	_____	• Do you serve as a peacemaker within the congregation?
_____	_____	_____	• Do you maintain a consistent Christian life-style in the presence of your family?
_____	_____	_____	• Do you try to live a disciplined and self-controlled life (what you read, listen to, view, and talk about)?
_____	_____	_____	• Do you live a life of joy?
_____	_____	_____	• Do you regularly spend quality time with God in prayer and Bible study?

Now review your answers. Based on what you see, complete the following statement: Regarding my involvement in the church, I need to

____.

In the Group

1. Report on the activity you planned to do with your wife or family: What did you decide to do? How did it work out? (Each member should do this.)
2. What's next? How can you continue improving your marriage and family life? (Optional: Consider doing another activity in this area for next week.)
3. Review your personal evaluation above. Tell the group your conclusion regarding your church involvement. Based on that conclusion, what action do you need to take? (Each member should do this.)
4. How can you honor your pastor(s)? As a group, think of some specific ways you might do that. Then select one your group can do in the next week.
5. Close your time by praying for your pastor(s).

Memory Verse: "The elders who direct the affairs of the church well are worthy of double honor, especially those whose work is preaching and teaching" (1 Tim. 5:17).

On Your Own

1. Follow through on your group plan to honor your pastor.
2. Optional: Do another activity designed to strengthen your marriage or fathering.
3. Read Promise 6, "A Man and His Brothers," before the next meeting.

Promise 6

A *Man* *and* His *Brothers*

A Promise Keeper is committed to reaching beyond any racial and denominational barriers to demonstrate the power of biblical unity.

PROMISE 6

Introduction

The Body of Christ comprises a wide diversity of members. There are many denominations, various styles of worship, and representatives from all walks of life. Those differences frequently produce tension. People who are different from us tend to make us feel uncomfortable. We'd prefer to stay close to those we know, in a style with which we are comfortable. But is that the biblical mandate?

This tension goes back to the church in its earliest form, as shown in the book of Acts. Soon after Jesus left this earth, the first Gentiles—that is, non-Jews—made professions of faith. Immediately there was tension between the Jews, with their clearly defined forms of worship, and the Gentiles, who often emerged out of pagan rituals and had no history of worshiping the one true God.

Today, similar tension persists. We see it between the different races, who rarely mingle in worship (or anywhere else). We see it between denominations and theological persuasions. But the Bible says there is only one Body. Jesus prayed that we all might be one. As men who are Promise Keepers, we must determine to break beyond the barriers and our comfort zones and get to know other members of that Body. For many, this will be uncomfortable. But the rewards are rich.

We introduce this topic with a chapter by Bill McCartney, founder of Promise Keepers and head coach of the University of Colorado football team. Coach McCartney walks us through the process he went through as his eyes were opened to the hurts and needs of his black brothers. And then Pastor Gordon England and Bishop Phillip Porter talk about how to reach out to meet those of different races and denominations. Bishop Porter and Pastor England live this message—their friendship crosses both denominational and racial lines.

A Call to Unity

by
Bill McCartney

It happened in the mid 1980s. I had been the football coach at Colorado University for a few years when a black Denver attorney by the name of Teddy Woods died at the age of 40. In his college days, Teddy had excelled as a student-athlete at C.U. Although he didn't play for me, I had met him and knew of his prowess and influence in the Denver area.

I arrived early for the funeral and found a seat in the front of the church. By the time the service began, the auditorium was full. Now, bear in mind that I didn't know the other people and had only met Teddy in passing. I was there to pay my respects because he had played football for C.U. and I was the current coach.

What happened to me that day changed my life. It may be hard for you to understand, but when I sat down and started listening to the music, I was deeply affected. The mournful singing of the mostly black congregation expressed a level of pain I hadn't seen or felt before. As I looked from side to side across the crowd, I realized that their grief over the loss of Teddy Woods was bringing to the surface an even deeper hurt. This wasn't just a funeral; it was also a gathering of wounded, long-suffering believers.

In response, I began to weep uncontrollably. I tried to cover my tears, fearing someone would see me and recognize that I barely knew Teddy Woods. I thought they might accuse me of grandstanding to gain acceptance and approval in the inner city—a recruiting ploy. Yet I couldn't hold the tears back. The grieving and groaning exceeded anything I had ever experienced. I have never been the same since then.

I had come in touch, for the first time, with the pain, struggle, despair, and anguish of the black people. Stunned by that experience, I felt a great desire to understand what I had observed. I also wanted to pursue what I had felt in my spirit. Although Boulder, the city where I live, is 98 percent white, I work with black athletes and fellow coaches every day. I visit the homes of many black families during recruiting season every year. And I had a sense that God was calling me to a deeper understanding of their lives that would greatly influence me both personally and in my role as a leader of Promise Keepers.

So I began to question black people I had known for years. It amazed me that despite wide differences in their ages and the places where they had grown up, they all identified directly with the pain I had felt in the church that day. They told stories about dramatic experiences and everyday examples of the injustices they face as black Americans.

One black clergyman, for instance, told of a gang shooting in which an innocent 12-year-old boy had been killed. The boy and his family were active participants in his church. When the news of the boy's death got out, the pastor almost doubled over in pain, so great was his grief. Many black leaders called or wrote to offer prayers and condolences, some from great distances. But nearby white leaders made no effort at all to express concern. The pastor was left with the clear impression that they simply didn't care.

A good friend who is not a Christian told me plainly why he doesn't believe in the "white man's God." As a child in the South, he knew he was not welcome in the all-white church on the corner. He would stand outside, near a window, during services and listen to the preacher speak about love, all the time knowing there was no love in that church for him.

At one point, this same friend witnessed a Ku Klux Klan rally in which the speaker held up a monkey's skull and claimed it was an exact replica of a black man's head. Can you imagine the rage mixed with fear that my friend felt that night? Can you understand why that night remains vivid and powerful in his memory?

The night before C.U.'s second game of the 1993 football season, we were in Texas preparing to play Baylor the next afternoon. To help the guys relax, I had arranged for our traveling squad to watch the Whitaker-Chavez championship prizefight that evening. Chavez's record was 88-0. Whitaker, a black man, had fought half as many matches with only one loss.

Seventy of us gathered in a small room to watch the bout. Approximately half were black. I sat back and observed my players closely. Virtually all the black kids were pulling for Whitaker; the white kids seemed evenly divided between Whitaker and Chavez. The black players were clearly more animated, often cheering and jumping to their feet, while the white players were generally more subdued. I was intrigued by the difference in culture.

Whitaker appeared to be in control throughout the fight, and the TV announcers spoke of his big edge over and over. Even though both boxers were still standing when the bout ended after 12 rounds, the winner seemed clear. We were all sure Whitaker had given Chavez his first defeat.

There was a delay, however, in totaling the judges' scorecards. The TV commentators said, "Could they possibly award this fight to Chavez? Surely not."

A hush came over our room. You could sense that the black players began to fear the worst. And when the ring announcer said that the fight was a draw—no winner—there was no protest in our ranks. Everyone filed out of the room quietly. The feeling was clear in the eyes and body language of our black young men: Injustice again. The black fighter has to knock out his opponent to win—he will never get the benefit of a decision.

Then there's the clear case of one of my assistant coaches at C.U. This man is smart, talented, a good teacher of the game, a skilled recruiter. In short, he has all the ingredients of a successful head coach. From a selfish standpoint, I'd like him to stay right where he is, because he's a friend and a tremendous asset to our program. I also know that if he went to another school as the head coach, his team would beat mine a fair share of the time!

The simple fact is, however, that no one has offered him a head coaching job. Why? Because he's black. There's no doubt whatsoever in my mind that if he were white, he would have been a head coach somewhere years ago.

The Call to Unity

Why do I tell these stories, hoping you'll feel at least a little of what I feel? Why is the issue of racial (and denominational) reconciliation so important to Promise Keepers that we're asking you to make a commitment to it? Let me explain in two ways.

First, the issue is vital because the Bible reveals clearly that it's the will of Almighty God for His people to be united. Jesus said to the Father, "I pray also for those who will believe in me through their message, that all of them may be one, Father, just as you are in me and I am in you. . . . May they be brought to complete unity to let the world know that you sent me and have loved them even as you have loved me" (John 17:20-23).

The apostle Paul wrote, "For we were all baptized by one Spirit into one body" (1 Cor. 12:13).

When the New Testament church struggled with the threat of division between believing Jews and Gentiles—two racial groups that generally despised each other in that time and place—Paul wrote the following corrective in Ephesians 2:13-16:

> In Christ Jesus you who were once far away have been brought near through the blood of Christ. For he himself is our peace, who has made the two one and has destroyed the barrier, the dividing wall of hostility, by abolishing in his flesh the law with its commandments and regulations. His purpose was to create in himself one new man out of the two, thus making peace, and in this one body to reconcile both of them to God through the cross, by which he put to death their hostility.

If I understand those passages and others like them correctly, divisions should not exist among Christians. But we know that's not the case. We are divided along racial and denominational lines.

The second reason reconciliation is so important to Promise Keepers grows out of an incident that occurred at one of our first conferences, in 1991. "Only" about 4,000 of us were gathered that year, but we already had dreams of filling Folsom Field with 50,000 men in the near future. As I got up to address the men at the end of that conference, I looked out over the crowd, and I noticed that it was overwhelmingly white. The absence of men of color somehow hit me between the eyes, and in that moment, the Spirit of God clearly said to my spirit, "You can fill that stadium, but if men of other races aren't there, I won't be there, either."

That message, which has since been confirmed in various ways to all the leaders of Promise Keepers, was the beginning of our understanding that the building of bridges across the divisions that currently separate believers is an important part of why God called us into being as an organization. It may be our most difficult mission, but I'm convinced that it's essential.

What will happen if Promise Keepers begin to reach out across racial and denominational lines? One strong possibility is the outbreak of revival in

America. You see, I believe racism and denominational divisions have done more than just about anything to hamper the church's witness to the world. So many people of color, like the friend I mentioned earlier, have been totally turned off to the God we proclaim by our obvious lack of love. Even nonbelieving white people know that Christians are supposed to love and that far too often we fail to do so. This is why I'm certain that revival can't take place until the church grows far more united in obedience to God's command.

On the other hand, I'm equally convinced that if we take this promise seriously and begin the process of reconciliation, incredible things are possible for the kingdom of God. Think back to the story of the early days of the church in Acts 2. The church was born on the Day of Pentecost, when people from many countries, cultures, and (no doubt) races heard the gospel in their own languages and believed in the Lord Jesus. Then, we read beginning in verse 42, those new Christians met regularly to eat together, to fellowship, to pray, and to worship God. Those who had possessions gave joyfully and sacrificially to meet the needs of those who lacked. And what was the result of this display of loving unity? The church "enjoy[ed] the favor of all the people. And the Lord added to their number daily those who were being saved" (v. 47).

Imagine how the world would respond to a church that was truly one in spirit. To be sure, we would face some opposition. Racism is Satan's stronghold, after all, one of his best tools for breeding hatred and undermining the work of the church, and he won't give up easily. But many thousands—if not millions—would be drawn to such a fellowship, such a demonstration of the power of God's love, just as they were 2,000 years ago.

Imagine what a united church could do with the gang problem in our country; with the need for young people in single-parent homes to have positive role models, heroes, and hopes for a better tomorrow; with the lack of educational and employment opportunities for certain segments of our society. I believe the kind of unity in the Body of Christ that we're talking about could unleash the fantastic potential God has given us to make a positive difference that no one else can possibly make. The unifying of godly people of all colors in contrast to racism would be an undeniable witness of His grace.

Now, I don't mean to suggest that all cultural differences and denominational distinctives are going to disappear. But what I know is that Almighty God wants to bring Christian men together regardless of their ethnic origin, denominational background, or style of worship. There's only one criterion for this kind of unity: to love Jesus and be born of the Spirit of God. Can we look one another in the eye—black, white, red, brown, yellow, Baptist, Presbyterian, Assemblies of God, Catholic, and so on—and get together on this common ground: "We believe in salvation through Christ alone, and we have made Him the Lord of our lives"? Is that not the central, unifying reality of our existence? And if it is, can we not focus on that and call each other brother instead of always emphasizing our differences? Men, we have to get together on this!

The Sin of Racism

Perhaps you look at the issue of racism and denominational divisiveness and say, "That's not me! I don't hate anybody, and I don't take responsibility for the plight of people of color." Or, "I can't be responsible for what happened hundreds of years ago. I wasn't there." If that's the case, let me ask you to rethink the issue in a couple of ways.

First, take the time and make the effort to *prayerfully* examine your heart. In God's presence, ask yourself questions like these: "Do I truly not consider myself better than people of one or more other races—more intelligent, creative, honest, hard-working, moral, trustworthy? How would I feel if a minority family sat next to me in church, invited my family to a picnic in a public park, or moved in next door? How would I react if my Sunday school teacher or my child's teacher were a person of another race? How about if my new boss were a person of color? How would I respond if my child married someone of a different race?"

As you ask yourself such questions, keep in mind these words given by the Holy Spirit of God through the apostle John: "If anyone says, 'I love God,' yet hates his brother, he is a liar. For everyone who does not love his brother, whom he has seen, cannot love God, whom he has not seen. And he [God] has given us this command: Whoever loves God must also love his brother" (1 John 4:20-21).

Then, as you lay your heart open to God, deal with any traces of racism you find there according to 1 John 1:9, and ask Him to begin the process of changing your mind and heart.

Second, even if you have a clear conscience before God with regard to racism, there is a biblical principle that says we bear some responsibility for the unrepented sins of our forefathers. Let me explain.

The Old Testament clearly shows a continuity of God's dealing with His people, generation after generation. This may have been blessing upon blessing or judgment for a prolonged period of years, even multiple generations.

Second Samuel 21, for example, shows how God called Israel to accountability under the reign of King David for a breach of integrity under King Saul, David's predecessor. Saul had broken a covenant with God by not sparing the Gibeonites after he and Israel had sworn to do so, and David's generation suffered the judgment: "During the reign of David, there was a famine for three successive years; so David sought the face of the LORD. The LORD said, 'It is on account of Saul and his blood-stained house; it is because he put the Gibeonites to death' " (v. 1).

What Saul did was a direct parallel to "ethnic cleansing" in our day. (Ethnic cleansing is racism without the restraint of law.) Because of his sin, God judged Israel with a sustained famine for three years. The acknowledgment of that sin and restitution to the surviving Gibeonites was necessary before the judgment was lifted. "After that, God answered prayer in behalf of the land" (v. 14).

In another biblical account, Daniel pleaded with the Lord in prayer and fasting because he understood that Jerusalem would suffer desolation for 70 years for the sins of his generation and the generations of his forefathers (see Dan. 9:4-19). In verse 16 he said, "Our sins and the iniquities of our fathers have made Jerusalem and your people an object of scorn to all those around us."

Most Americans live in a "now only" mentality. But the historic cultures of the world present a radical alternative to this thinking and help us understand the biblical principle of generational sin. The Chinese, for example, tend to take a long look at their history. For them, things change slowly. They see their own lives integrally linked to their national ethnic history spanning millennia. Europeans criticize Americans for being ignorant of world history, and even their own history.

Not only do we tend to be ignorant of the biblical principle involved here, but we also just don't like it. To our highly individualistic way of thinking, it doesn't seem fair. But God is not bound by our sense of fairness, and the biblical principle stands.

Less than a century and a half ago, the forefathers of our contemporary black brothers and sisters were being treated as subhuman animals, property to be chained and whipped, bought and sold, by many of our white forefathers. Have we in the white church ever repented of that sin to any significant extent? No, we have not. We've stood against a lot of other social evils, but we have not stood against racism and called it what it is: sin! We have been divided by racism, staying silent, acting with, at best, only token resistance.

We should feel conviction deep in our souls for this sin. The damage is incalculable. The toll is immeasurable. We should drop to our knees before Almighty God in repentance.

Because God reconciled us to Himself through His only Son, Jesus Christ, we *are going to reconcile* with our Christian brothers of different races, cultures, and denominations. We're going to break down the walls that separate us so that we might demonstrate the power of biblical unity based on what we have in common: our love for Jesus and our connectedness through Him. We will live for one purpose: to bring glory to the name of Jesus Christ and to fulfill the desires of God's heart.

First Steps

I don't know of any way to achieve this reconciliation apart from Jesus Christ. Only His Spirit can break down the walls that separate Christians. Matthew 22:37-40 sums up our strategy: " 'Love the Lord your God with all your heart and with all your soul and with all your mind.' This is the first and greatest commandment. And the second is like it: 'Love your neighbor as yourself.' All the Law and the Prophets [i.e., the entire Old Testament] hang on these two commandments." Love God and love your neighbor. That's the bottom line. In the words of Paul,

> Let no debt remain outstanding, except the continuing debt to love one another, for he who loves his fellowman has fulfilled the law. The commandments, "Do not commit adultery," "Do not murder," "Do not steal," "Do not covet," and whatever other commandment there may be, are summed up in this one rule: "Love your neighbor as yourself." Love does no harm to its neighbor. Therefore love is the fulfillment of the law. (Rom. 13:8-10)

Biblical love and unity do not come at an easy price. They require us to lay down our lives for our friends (see John 15:13), to leave our self-centeredness and enlarge our circle of understanding so we can appreciate another's history and experiences. They demand that we become good listeners and share the pain of those who have been hurt by past domination. They oblige us to seek forgiveness for the sins of our fathers and for the same racial oppression that continues to this day. They require that we endure confrontations and crises until we establish trust in one another.

This kind of love means that we come together in our common poverty, weaknesses, and sins to receive God's riches, strength, and grace—together. It means we allow God to replace our personal prejudices with His perspective. It compels us to accept the essential value of every person, understanding that we need each other to be complete:

> But God has combined the members of the body and has given greater honor to the parts that lacked it, so that there should be no division in the body, but that its parts should have equal concern for each other. If one part suffers, every part suffers with it; if one part is honored, every part rejoices with it. (1 Cor. 12:24-26)

If our hearts are right before God and our motive is love, He will show us the way. The plan I'm proposing starts with prayer, then calls for genuine, real relationship with brothers of different ethnic and denominational heritages.

1. Pray.

Can you imagine what might happen if every church identified a point person to lead a prayer posse in that congregation? I challenge you to begin by making that a goal in your church and to pray for the following:

First, pray that your pastor will see through the darkness of a divided church to the light of a unified Body of Christ. Pray that he will address the problem of racism vigorously and lead his congregation in repentance.

Second, pray that the hearts in your congregation will soften. Pray that they will become educated about the sin of racism and begin to bear the burden of pain that their brothers and sisters of color have endured. Pray that this effort will be sustained and not a one-time venture.

Third, pray for your community to address the problem of racism. The inner cities and slums need resources to help lift them out of total apathy. We need to dissolve the gangs. All of this is possible because Jesus wants to do it.

Godly men must be impassioned with righteous determination to make amends. Society tries in vain. Government efforts are losing ground. Defeat swallows mankind's best ideas. May every church plead in unison for God's heart and God's solution to bring reconciliation. May our prayer warriors work overtime. Let the pulse of the Body of Christ quicken and not rest until we see change. And let it begin with you and me.

2. Pursue genuine relationships with Christian men of different races and denominations.

Our hearts will not break for our brethren until we enter into relationship with them. I suggest that you begin by establishing groups of men who are committed to living as Promise Keepers. Find at least two other guys from your church who share this vision. From there, look around and find a few brothers from different denominational and ethnic heritages with whom you can start to build a relationship of trust and honor. You might meet these men at a local Promise Keepers breakfast, at work, at the Y, or in your neighborhood as you and they are out walking your dogs or playing catch with your kids.

The men may be from one church or several. You may meet in groups at work, in a restaurant, in a church, or in a home. Keep the agenda simple. Share insight and wisdom from the pages of Scripture. Understand each other's pain and victories. And pray for one another.

Make a concerted effort to get below the surface in those relationships. Let me explain why that's so important. I know two guys, one black and one white, who are nearly inseparable. You can see them together on any given day. They work together. They laugh and clown around. They hug and embrace. They sing and harmonize. They claim to be best friends.

One day while I was with them, I asked the black man, "Have you ever told your best friend how you really feel about being black, about the pain and resentment, about the smoldering hostility for white people deep in your spirit?"

"No," he said.

"Is it there?" I asked.

"Yes," he answered.

Those two men had something good going. However, until a man hurts as his brother hurts, they don't really know each other. How can you pray for someone when you don't know his deepest pain? When you do know his pain, you have real relationship.

As one missionary said, "I don't know how to love the poor except one at a time." We can embrace that same wisdom in overcoming hostility and division in the body of Christ—one relationship at a time. But beware! If a man of color doesn't trust you right away, remember that you may represent hundreds of years of oppression and mistrust to him. Stay with it. Keep trying; keep reaching out in love. Ask God to work in the hearts of everyone involved.

Micah 6:8 is a profound Scripture. This is what God requires of us: "To act justly and to love mercy and to walk humbly with your God." It sounds simple enough. However, when I looked into the verse, I discovered that it meant something entirely different from how it originally appeared to me.

"Act justly" means to see the need in others and respond to it. To "love mercy" always triumphs over judgment. And to "walk humbly with your God" means that we agree with what God says as opposed to what man says.

God requires that we see the need in our brethren and respond. If we do, His very heart will go with us.

Taking the Next Step

by
Phillip Porter and Gordon England

How did you feel about what Coach McCartney wrote in the preceding chapter? Angry? Uncomfortable? Unsure what to do next? He issued a tough challenge.

Why in the world did Promise Keepers select "racial and denominational barriers" when it focused on Christian unity? The primary reason is our sense that the Lord led us to embrace this truth. We must be obedient.

Alone we can't change much; you can't, either. But together, with a million other brothers—committed Promise Keepers—we can influence a nation. We can demonstrate that what history, the political process, and the legal system could not do, faith, obedience, repentance, and unity in Jesus Christ *can* change.

The body of Christ is different from the culture in general. The world system is not designed to conform to the will of God. As citizens of all races, we should hope for respect, dignity, and opportunity for one another. But the Body of Christ is called to a higher standard—not mere tolerance, but love such as Christ has for you.

Consider this: Whoever loves God must also love his brother (see 1 John 4:19-21). The Bible is clear about that. What does it mean? We might say that it is impossible to truly love Jesus Christ more than we love the man we love the least! Now, that's a sobering thought.

Perhaps our own journey will encourage you. Both of us are in ministry in the Denver area, Phil as a bishop in his denomination, Gordon as pastor of a suburban church. However, we'd never met prior to a planning meeting for a Concert of Prayer. During our time of discussion, Phil, a black man, was asked to give his testimony. He told about coming to southern Colorado to take a job as a social worker in 1959. He was fresh out of Phillips University in Oklahoma with a letter confirming his job. But his employer was shocked when he arrived. The agency was unaware that Phillips had any black students. "There's no job here for you!" he was told. Too hurt and ashamed to return to Oklahoma, Phil took a bus to Denver, where he got a job as a cook in order to provide for his family.

Gordon, who is white, had known many blacks but had never met a person of Phil's stature who, in abject honesty, had divulged such pain, yet with a loving spirit. When Phil finished his testimony, it seemed only appropriate for Gordon to apologize for that wrong and to ask for forgiveness on behalf of those from Gordon's race who had sinned against Phil. The meeting ended with tears and prayer, and the forging of a brotherhood had begun.

Does it really matter whether Christian men are seeking unity? We think the importance is clear from Jesus' prayer in John 17: Those who are His *must* be one, even as God the Father and Jesus the Son are one. It is this unity, Jesus said, that will show the world the reality of God's love.

As someone has said, the idea of unity is to create a salad, not a stew. God has made a world of people different from one another, even within denominational and ethnic groups. Gender, age, personality, ability, physical characteristics, appearance, talent, and interests are but a few of the specific points of diversity.

Some people say they don't see color. But unless they're blind, they're probably trying to be nice and say race is not an issue. In either case, they're wrong. For example, the authors of this chapter, Phil Porter and Gordon England, are different racially. Both are okay, both are unique, but clearly they are *not* the same. Yet each adds flavor to the Body of Christ. Lettuce, tomatoes, cucumbers, and bell peppers are all different in appearance, taste, and texture, but all are good together in a salad. If this is hard to accept, run all your food through the blender for a month and you'll get the point.

Okay, then, what do we do? If we're convinced that God desires unity among all believers, each of us needs to reach out to brothers who are of different denominational or ethnic backgrounds. Coach McCartney has outlined the biblical mandate and issued the challenge. How do we go about this? We suggest four things.

1. Relationships with brothers begin in the heart.

Reaching out begins with conviction by God's Spirit about sin in our attitudes and behavior. Sin is not ethnic specific. We all have probably, at some time, experienced hate, bad attitudes, or even just the emotional scum of feeling somehow better than another. That needs to be dealt with. Recognize it. Admit it. Confess it to the Lord. Then confess it to any we have specifically sinned against.

Gordon didn't *have* to ask for Phil's forgiveness that day they met. Gordon didn't personally offend Phil 30 years earlier. However, Gordon recognized the pain of that experience, and in the interest of building a bridge and helping to heal the hurt of his new friend, he bore the burden of Phil's pain and asked for forgiveness. That act was the beginning of their fellowship. It was an act of humility that opened the door to healing and relationship.

Repentance is an active choice we can each make. We can choose to acknowledge the reality of historic sin and the ongoing existence of prejudice in every ethnic group. The fact that others are also "to blame" does not lessen our responsibility to hear from the Lord and to deal, as He convicts us, with our part. For example, I (Gordon) was raised in a home that had little classic bigotry, but over the past 50 years, I've heard innumerable ethnic jokes. A small percentage were clever and funny, but the vast majority had a demeaning, derogatory, and hurtful twist.

What could possibly motivate men to repeat those jokes? There are plenty of other good stories available. I must admit—perhaps you will also—that if you degrade another person or group, you take yourself off the hook to treat them well. But that's certainly not the Golden Rule—treating others as you'd want to be treated.

As a young black man of about 15 growing up in Enid, Oklahoma, I (Phillip) remember an experience that taught me about forgiveness. My father and I had gone into a grocery store some distance from the "Negro" district, as it was called then. As my dad bent down to look at an item on a bottom shelf, a man came up behind him and kicked him—a solid boot! Dad was a good-sized man, and I was already well-developed and a successful boxer. When Dad was kicked, I was shocked but waited to see what he would do. He straightened up slowly and deliberately, then turned toward the assailant, who blurted out that he had wanted to "kick his butt" for a long time. I could feel myself getting angry. I was ready to square off with the guy. After all, my dad and I were both there; we could put a hurt on this guy.

But Dad, a "tent-making" pastor, looked the guy straight on with strength and poise and said, "As long as you're a white man and I'm a black man, don't you ever do that again." Then he turned to me and said, "No! We're going," and we walked out together to the car. There Dad told me that guys like that didn't see us as people. They were ignorant and afraid. We could be angry and bitter, or we could forgive them because they didn't know what they were doing. We could leave that hurt with God. He would take the offense and leave us free in our spirit. Over my years as a pastor, I've often reflected on the same words of forgiveness our Savior spoke concerning His tormentors.

The result of repentance, apology, forgiveness requested, and forgiveness granted is a reconciled relationship.

2. Relationship is a process.

The process of building a relationship across old barriers is a "going deeper" kind of experience. It moves from the surface, the generalizations, to the specific; from the comfortable, good feelings of initial obedience to understanding and, through understanding, to the pain of the other. To willingly accept a trip into another's pain seems masochistic or stupid. However, it is a precursor to blessing. Just as the apostle Paul called us to be identified with the suffering of Christ, he also promised that we will share in His glory.

To develop a truly open, reconciled relationship—be it with a man of a different race, your wife, a child, or any other person—is to be personally and spiritually enlarged. This is the basis of the interdependency of the Body of Christ. Conversely, in isolation we are incomplete. We are joined to the Head, Jesus Christ, but we are missing body parts.

Several years ago, a friend of Gordon's suffered a stroke that left him paralyzed on the left side. He said it was as if he had lost his arm and leg — in fact maybe worse, because he still had to carry them around but they would not function. Through bold, tenacious discipline in therapy and the prayers of family and the church, however, he was restored to nearly full function. The pleasure and excitement to this man of effectively "adding an arm and a leg" was thrilling.

Reconciliation can bring us the same kind of joy as we experience all the parts of Christ's Body. Jesus modeled this when "for the joy set before him [He] endured the cross" (Heb. 12:2).

Can you be a bridge builder? Many Promise Keepers are currently asking that question. The answer is that you can have a part. If your spirit is saying "Yes!" you fit the first category of bridge builders—those who demonstrate a heart for others.

If you aren't sure how to start, you might begin with a Promise Keepers event—perhaps a breakfast—where you can meet men of different denominations and cultures in your community.

Some of the men from my (Gordon's) suburban, largely white church meet with a group from a couple of inner-city churches. This has become meaningful to our guys and, I hope, also to the men from the inner city. At one of the early Saturday-morning sessions, we were still introducing ourselves, talking of our families or our jobs. Then a man named John from our group quietly and honestly said, "I'm trying to learn some new skills and get back into the job market." He had been out of work since defense-industry cutbacks eliminated his job. When he said he was unemployed, every inner-city guy turned toward him. It seemed there was surprise and immediate support for him—surprise that a sharp, professional-looking white guy could be unemployed, and support because even though this guy didn't have a job, he still would get up early and drive into the city to show he had a heart to be a bridge builder.

The process of building relationships will also be aided if you or others in your group already have cross-cultural experience. This may have been through a job, the military, athletics, or a college roommate. The value of this exposure is not that it makes you a cultural expert, but it probably showed you that others don't see you the same way you see yourself or your cultural tradition. It informs you of others and of the inaccuracies of your perceptions.

Traveling and living in other places also facilitate bridge building. Just being where things are different or seeing situations through fresh eyes will increase a person's willingness to accept different ways of doing things. (We all tend to think that if our way isn't the only way, at least it's the best way.)

When we change our perspective, we open ourselves to the possibility that our world may have been too small. We realize that our prejudice was unfounded or at least not well founded. To lead in bridge building, we need to be open to learning and expanding our horizons.

The ability to speak a second language will also help in bridge building. Language and culture are not the same, but many nuances of culture are reflected in the idioms of the language. This is another key to expanded perspective. It may be a tool, too, for direct and meaningful communication in another person's native tongue.

Yes, you can be a bridge builder if you have a heart for others. And it will help if you have experience cross-culturally, have traveled or lived in other places, are married to a person of a different ethnic background, or speak a second language. Jesus was a bridge builder from heaven to earth—He became a man, spoke our language, and is calling for Himself a bride out of every tongue, nation, and tribe.

3. Develop a plan.

The cliché that says "people don't plan to fail, they just fail to plan" is true with groups as well as individuals. Planning is essential in groups, because without a plan, it's impossible to share the vision and get people to become involved.

Prayer is the single most important part of the plan. Activists would say, "Never mind, let the elderly women pray. We need to be involved!" But we say, "Not so fast." People have been trying to fix through natural means a problem that started in sin. Separation and alienation go clear back to Genesis 3.

Prayer and reconciliation are the two greatest needs of the church. The lack of prayer robs us of the power of God. The absence of reconciliation robs the church of the power of unity! To break down the barriers of historic sin, both the sin of racism and the sin of resentment, we need God's power. So start the plan with prayer. Pray first for passion and commitment, then pray for conviction and repentance.

This initial step will make you ready to start involving others of differing backgrounds. It's probably best for your group to reach out to one other group. Caution! Don't go any further until you start to build relationships. Don't set an agenda other than that you want to establish a relationship based in the Lord Jesus Christ and with a goal of being reconciled to Christian brothers. Do not set an activity agenda or a five-year plan—yet.

Make it your pattern to do things *with* one another, not for, to, or in spite of one another. The early period of relationship building needs to be for getting acquainted, building trust, and letting personal bonding occur. As Christian man to Christian man, start praying together. Pray for each other and for one another's families. Pray for direction in the shared relationship.

Also, have some fun! Eat together, go to a ball game, or whatever. The relationship needs to be real and broad and touch several areas of life, not just church. When a sense of loyalty and interest is developing on both sides of the ethnic aisle, then it's time to start doing further planning. When what started as "oughta" turns to "wanta," you know you're on track.

What makes a relationship grow? Keeping at it. Phil observes about Gordon that "he keeps comin' at ya" and doesn't give up. That tenacity works both ways. Just recently, when we had been apart for about three weeks due to travel and business in our churches, Phil called Gordon just to see how he was doing. No needs, no projects, no advice, just a brother affirming another out of mutual love.

Humor is a must! All guys will make mistakes, and it's wonderful to be able to lighten up a bit with each other. This is especially helpful when you're wrong. Phil laughs with Gordon (he could laugh at him often) when he blows it. It's easy to think you know how the other guy or all people of the other race feel. Your brother may realize that you're off base and don't have a clue. Humor can open up the conversation, kindly removing your foot from your mouth.

Prayer has been a vital part of our friendship. Prayer is a vulnerable activity. In sincerity, if you strip away all pretense before God, you can also be real with one another. We pray together about our kids, our churches, and Promise Keepers. It's not always convenient—we live across the city from one another. But when we pray together, the bond grows between us, and the motivation to pray for each other increases when we're apart.

Understanding will help break down fear or stereotyping. A great resource can be books on the subject of reconciliation. Tapes by key leaders are good discussion starters. Relaxed dialogue will allow individuals in both groups to gain insight. People in both groups will learn not only from the other group's insight, but also from hearing members of their own group speak.

If the opportunity affords itself, your new cross-racial group may choose to take on a project related to one of the churches or perhaps reaching out to help someone else. There is something very bonding about men working together. Often we let down our guard and become more vulnerable when laboring alongside someone.

Keep the relationship-building issue on the front burner, but don't be in a hurry! Each person is starting at a different place of readiness. Plan periodic opportunities for new men to become involved, but reduce the walk-in, walk-out syndrome as much as possible.

4. Be ready to change and to give generously as you learn.

Reading the story of Zacchaeus in Luke 19, you wonder what Paul Harvey would say if he told the rest of the story! Zacchaeus was a sinner according to both the crowd around him and Jesus. His scam was exploiting his countrymen for personal gain. As if Roman rule wasn't bad enough for a Jewish businessman, here was a turncoat who would collect all he could get from the victimized subject, give the government only what he had to, and pocket the rest.

Zacchaeus was rich, but he must have been empty inside. Somehow he overheard the truth about this prophet Jesus. His curiosity was so intense that he did a most unusual thing. This short but fully grown man climbed up a tree! Little boys climb trees when at play. Put it in our terms—a collection agent pulls his Lexus over to the curb, jumps up to grab a branch, and, still in his three-piece suit, pulls himself up so he can look over the crowd surrounding a street preacher as it moves down the avenue toward him.

It didn't take a lot of preaching on Jesus' part, perhaps none, to convince Zacchaeus of his need. Maybe it was the truth that another person had told him about this Jesus and His call for mercy and justice. That truth may have been like the statement of Billy Graham for us that racism is the greatest sin of our land. Anyway, he was ready to respond. He had a change of heart. From his personal greed, he addressed others' need.

The poor—do you care about them? Do you see them as a nuisance and maybe even like nonpeople? Zacchaeus gave 50 percent of what he had! Give us a break! Did you notice that the tax collector didn't even stop to see if he could get an IRS deduction? For some of us, that's not a change of heart, that's a cardiac arrest! Then he paid restitution for the wrong he had done. He was speaking about individual people he had ripped off. He knew who they were and what he had taken. He doubtless had two sets of books.

How does that fit the modern American scene? We submit that the rip-off we can all identify is the lack of access to the economic mainstream for inner-city minorities. We're not talking about charity, welfare, or the dole. But what would happen if every Christian man who had the power or opportunity would take a man outside the economic loop and pull him in? Mentor, help, affirm, guide, and in every way possible insure that the one who had been denied an opportunity got a chance to succeed? Do you think that person would also be interested in knowing our Jesus?

This "Zacchaean" pattern of sin to repentance, greed to need, and restitution for wrong puts substance to the words of James 2:18: "I will show you my faith by what I do."

Rather than try to rationalize or skirt around it, a man of integrity will say, "Yes, I see it. I'll repent in my heart, ask God for forgiveness, and ask for forgiveness from my ethnic brother."

Forgiveness is an unconditional choice! And it's God's call to those who have been offended; they can decide to be obedient to the Lord Jesus and forgive. This forgiveness is not based on preconditions. It's also not based on assumed future favor. It doesn't even depend on the offending party's desire to be reconciled, but rather on the offended party's desire to live openly before the Lord and not be burdened with the weight of unresolved sin or the sin of resentment.

That's what it's all about. Take the risk! Step out in prayer and faith, and see what God will do as you obey and the Body of Christ is unified.

A Man and His Brothers
Personal Evaluation

On a scale from 1 to 10, with 1 meaning "I could never do that" and 10 being "total enthusiasm," rate yourself on the following statements:

1. I am ready and willing to meet with brothers in Christ from other denominations. _____
2. I am ready and willing to meet with brothers in Christ from other ethnic and cultural backgrounds. _____

What concerns might you have about meeting with brothers from other races?

In the Group

1. What did you do to honor your pastor last week? How did it go? How did your pastor respond?
2. What were your thoughts as you read through Coach McCartney's chapter?
3. As you think about reaching across denominational or racial barriers, what are your biggest concerns?
4. How can you take the first step to establish relationships with brothers of different denominational or ethnic backgrounds?
5. Close with prayer. You might look at Christ's prayer in John 17:20-24. Pray for the unity of the Body of Christ and the part God would have you play in helping bring that about. Pray for at least one other church in the community. And pray for your brothers in another ethnic group in your area—that God would open the doors for relationship and reconciliation.

Memory Verse: "I pray also for those who will believe in me through their message, that all of them may be one, Father, just as you are in me and I am in you. May they also be in us so that the world may believe that you have sent me" (John 17:20-21).

On Your Own

1. Pray daily for unity among Christians in your community, and for the relationships God would have you form with brothers of different denominations or races.
2. Read the final section, "A Man and His World," before your next meeting.

PROMISE 7

A Man and His World

A Promise Keeper is committed to influencing his world, being obedient to the Great Commandment (see Mark 12:30-31) and the Great Commission (see Matt. 28:19-20).

PROMISE 7

Introduction

We've covered a great deal of ground in this book. We conclude our look at the seven promises of a Promise Keeper by examining the Great Commandment and the Great Commission of Jesus Christ.

In the first chapter, we look at the command to love. A Promise Keeper is committed to loving God first and then his neighbor as himself. That sounds good in theory, but all of us inevitably run into someone who is just, well, hard to love. It might be a work associate who isn't all that honest. It might be the criminal whose senseless act changed your life forever. It could be the neighbor across the street whose noisy life-style keeps you awake at 2:00 in the morning. Did Christ really expect us to love everyone?

The answer is yes. But there's a secret. You can't love these people in your own strength. Dr. Bill Bright, founder and president of Campus Crusade for Christ, challenges us with a message that has helped millions around the world find freedom to love even the most unlovely.

We conclude with the Great Commission, Christ's instructions to His disciples just prior to leaving the earth. He told them, and us through them, to go into all nations and make disciples. Each of us has a part to play in the Great Commission. And to tell us how is one of the world's great evangelists, Luis Palau. Luis has preached in 60 nations of the world and has preached to 11 million people. But he is quick to say that you don't have to be an eloquent speaker to bring people to the Lord. Every faithful Promise Keeper can play a part.

The Greatest Power Ever Known

by
Dr. Bill Bright

Two gifted attorneys had great professional animosity, even hatred, for one another. Even though they were distinguished members of the same firm, they were constantly criticizing and making life miserable for each other.

Then one of them came to Christ through our ministry, and some months later, he asked me for counsel. "I have hated and criticized my partner for years," he said, "and he has been equally antagonistic toward me. But now that I'm a Christian, I don't feel right about continuing our warfare. What do I do?"

"Why not ask your partner to forgive you and tell him you love him?" I suggested.

"I could never do that!" he said. "That would be hypocritical! I *don't* love him. How could I tell him I love him when I don't?"

That lawyer had put his finger squarely on one of the great challenges of the Christian life. On the one hand, everybody wants to be loved. Most psychologists agree that man's greatest need is to love and be loved. No barrier can withstand the mighty force of love. On the other hand, however, so many people never experience love. And many people don't know *how* to express it—especially to those with whom they're in conflict. But early in my walk with God, I made an exciting spiritual discovery that has enriched my life and the lives of tens of thousands of others. By learning and applying these truths, you, too, can discover the life-changing power of love. It is a principle I call "How to Love by Faith."

Five Truths about Love

There are three Greek words translated into the one English word *love*: *eros*, which suggests sensual desire and does not appear in the New Testament; *phileo*, which is used for friendship or love of one's friends or relatives and conveys a sense of loving someone because he is worthy of love; and *agape*, which is God's supernatural, unconditional love for you revealed supremely through our Lord's death on the cross for your sins. It is the supernatural love He wants to produce in you and through you to others by His Holy Spirit. *Agape* love is given because of the character of the person loving rather than because of the worthiness of the object of that love. Sometimes it is love "in spite of" rather than "because of."

How does this kind of love express itself? The apostle Paul gave us an excellent description:

> Love is patient, love is kind. It does not envy, it does not boast, it is not proud. It is not rude, it is not self-seeking, it is not easily angered, it keeps no record of wrongs. Love does not delight in evil but rejoices with the truth. It always protects, always trusts, always hopes, always perseveres. Love never fails. (1 Cor. 13:4-8)

Later Paul admonished, "Let love be your greatest aim" (1 Cor. 14:1, TLB). There are five vital truths about love that will help you understand the basis for loving by faith.

1. God loves you unconditionally.

God loves with *agape*, the love described in 1 Corinthians 13. His love is not based on performance. Christ loves you so much that while you were yet a sinner, He died for you (see Rom. 5:8).

The parable of the prodigal son illustrates God's continuing unconditional love for His children. A man's younger son asked his father for his share of the family estate, packed up his belongings, and took a trip to a distant land, where he wasted all his money on parties and prostitutes. About the time that his money was gone, a great famine swept over the land, and he began to starve. He finally came to his senses and realized his father's hired men at least had food to eat. So he decided to return home, admit he had sinned, and ask for a job.

While he was on the road and still a long distance away, his father saw him and was filled with loving pity. He ran to his son, embraced him, and kissed him. Just as the son started to make his confession, his father interrupted to instruct the servants to prepare a celebration! His lost child had repented and come home, and he was lovingly restored to full status as a son.

Even when you are disobedient like the prodigal son, God continues to love you, waiting for you to respond to His love and forgiveness.

Just how much does He love you? Jesus once prayed to the Father, ". . . so that the world will know you sent me and will understand that *you love them as much as you love me*" (John 17:23, TLB, emphasis added). Think of it! God loves you as much as He loves His only begotten Son, the Lord Jesus. What a staggering, overwhelming truth to comprehend! In fact, such love is beyond our ability to grasp with the mind, but it is not beyond our ability to experience with our hearts.

2. You are commanded to love.

On one occasion, a teacher of the law came to Jesus and asked, "Of all the commandments, which is the most important?"

Jesus replied, " 'Love the Lord your God with all your heart and with all your soul and with all your mind and with all your strength.' The second is this: 'Love your neighbor as yourself.' There is no commandment greater than these" (Mark 12:28-31).

Jesus also said, "There is a saying, 'Love your *friends* and hate your enemies.' But I say: Love your *enemies!* Pray for those who *persecute* you! In that way you will be acting as true sons of your Father in heaven. . . . If you love only those who love you, what good is that? Even scoundrels do that much" (Matt. 5:43-46).

When Christians begin to act like Christians and love God, their neighbors, their enemies, and especially their Christian brothers—regardless of color, race, or class—we will see in our time, as in the first century, a great transformation in the whole of society. People will marvel when they observe our love in the same way people marveled when they observed those first-century believers, saying, "How they love one another" (see Acts 2:44-47).

At one time in my Christian life, I was troubled over the command to love God and others so completely. How could I ever measure up to such a high standard? Two important considerations have helped me a great deal. First, I found the assurance in the Bible that God has already given us what we need: "We know how dearly God loves us, and we feel this warm love everywhere within us because God has given us the Holy Spirit to fill our hearts with his love" (Rom. 5:5, TLB).

Second, by meditating on the attributes of God and the wonderful things He has done and is doing for me, I find my love for Him growing. I love Him because He first loved me.

As for loving others, when we are vitally yoked to Christ and walking in the Spirit, loving God with all our hearts, souls, and minds, we will fulfill His command to love others as ourselves. The apostle Paul explained just how wise this command is:

> If you love your neighbor as much as you love yourself you will not want to harm or cheat him, or kill him or steal from him. And you won't sin with his wife or want what is his, or do anything else the Ten Commandments say is wrong. All ten are wrapped up in this one, to love your neighbor as you love yourself. Love does no wrong to anyone. That's why it fully satisfies all of God's requirements. It is the only law you need. (Rom. 13:9-10, TLB)

Love is also a sure sign of our discipleship. "All men will know that you are my disciples, if you love one another," Jesus said (John 13:35). Our doctrine should be sound. Our faith should be strong. But neither is a sign or testimony to the world of our discipleship. Only love is.

3. You cannot love in your own strength.

Just as surely as "those who are in the flesh cannot please God," so in your own strength you cannot love as you ought. How many times have you resolved to love someone? How often have you tried to manufacture some kind of positive, loving emotion toward another person for whom you felt nothing? It's impossible, isn't it?

By nature, people are not patient and kind. We are jealous, envious, and boastful. We are proud, haughty, selfish, and rude, and we demand our own way. We could never love others the way God loves us!

4. You can love with God's love.

It was God's kind of love that brought you to Christ. It is this kind of love that is able to sustain and encourage you each day. Through His love in you, you can bring others to Christ and minister to fellow believers as God has commanded.

How does this love enter your life? It becomes yours the moment you receive Jesus Christ and the Holy Spirit comes to indwell you. The Scripture says the "fruit of the Spirit is love" (Gal. 5:22). In other words, when you are controlled by the Spirit, one of the ways His presence is demonstrated is by an outpouring of *agape* love in your life.

Now, this may all sound good in theory, but how do you make God's love a practical reality in your experience? By resolutions? By self-imposed discipline? No. The only way to do it is explained in my final point.

5. You love by faith.

Everything about the Christian life is based on faith. You love by faith just as you received Christ by faith, just as you are filled with the Holy Spirit by faith, and just as you walk by faith.

But if the fruit of the Spirit is love, as we just saw, you may logically ask, "Isn't it enough to be filled with the Spirit?" That's true from God's point of view, but it will not always be true in your actual experience.

Many Christians have loved with God's love without consciously or specifically claiming it by faith. Yet, without being aware of the fact, they were, indeed, loving by faith. Hebrews 11:6 reminds us that "without faith it is impossible to please God." Clearly, then, there is no demonstration of God's love where there is no faith.

How, then, do we love by faith in a practical way? It works like this: We know God has commanded us to love. We also know He promised in 1 John 5:14-15 that if we ask anything according to His will, He hears and will answer us. So we ask according to His command (His will), and then we receive His love by faith according to His promise, knowing His promises are always true. Let me illustrate how this happens.

In one case, I was having trouble loving a fellow staff member. I wanted to love him, and I knew I was commanded to do so. But because of certain inconsistencies and personality differences, I found it difficult. Then the Lord reminded me of 1 Peter 5:7: "Let him have all your worries and cares, for he is always thinking about you and watching everything that concerns you" (TLB). So I decided to give the problem to Him and love the man by faith—to act lovingly toward him regardless of my feelings, depending on God's love and strength within.

An hour later, I received a letter from that very man, who had no possible way of knowing what I had just decided. In fact, his letter had been written the day before. The Lord had foreseen the change in me. This friend and I met that afternoon and had the most wonderful time of prayer and fellowship we had ever experienced together.

One evening in Chicago, I spoke to a crowded room of more than 1,300 college students. They seemed to hang on every word as I explained how to love by faith. Early the next morning, a young woman with sparkling eyes and face aglow came up to me and said, "My life changed last night. For many years I have hated my parents. I haven't seen them since I was 17, and now I am 22. I left home as a result of a quarrel five years ago and haven't written or talked to them since, though they have tried repeatedly to contact and encourage me to return home. I determined that I would never see them again.

"A few months ago, I became a Christian. Last night you told me how to love my parents, and I could hardly wait to get out of that meeting and call them. I now really love them with God's kind of love, and I can hardly wait to see them!"

Remember the lawyer whose story began this chapter? After he protested that he couldn't love his critical partner, I explained how God commands His children to love even their enemies and that we love His way as a choice of the will, which we exercise by faith. I read to him the part of 1 Corinthians 13 quoted above. "You will note," I said, "that each of these descriptions of love is not an expression of the emotions but of the will."

Together we knelt to pray, and my friend asked God's forgiveness for his critical attitude toward his law partner and claimed God's love for him by faith.

Early the next morning, my friend walked into his partner's office and announced, "Something wonderful has happened to me. I've become a Christian, and I've come to ask you to forgive me for all I've done to hurt you in the past and to tell you that I love you."

The partner was so surprised and convicted of his own sin that he, too, asked for forgiveness and said, "I would like to become a Christian. Would you show me what I need to do?"

Other examples are endless. God has an infinite supply of His divine, supernatural *agape* love for each of us. It is for us to claim, to grow on, to spread to others, and thus to reach hundreds and thousands of others for Christ.

God's love is the greatest power in the universe. It changed the course of history. It can change our world today. It can revolutionize your family, your neighborhood, your workplace, and your church. Nothing—absolutely nothing—can overcome it.

I encourage you to make a list of everyone whom you do not like and begin today to love them by faith. Include those people who have hurt you in the past. Pray for them. Ask for eyes to see them as Christ sees them. Act lovingly toward them no matter how you feel. We don't love people because they deserve to be loved—we love them because Christ commands it and empowers us to do so. Your relationships will change as God's love in you overflows to others. Further, you will be a channel of God's own life and power into this needy world, and loving by faith, you will please your loving Master. The greatest force in the world is love!

The Great Commission

by
Luis Palau

"Lord, I promise to help fulfill the Great Commission in my world for Your glory."

It's a gutsy commitment to make, no question about it. It's not one to make lightly, flippantly, or without counting the cost.

But *now* is the time to re-evangelize our world! And we men should lead the way—in our families, our churches, and our communities. I can think of no greater thrill than obeying the Lord in this area of personal involvement in and commitment to evangelism.

People Are Searching

A few weeks ago, a successful businessman came to a Bible study I was leading. As I spoke about having the assurance of eternal life through faith in Jesus Christ, I noticed he had tears in his eyes.

On the way out, this man and I talked about the companies he owns. When the elevator stopped at the floor occupied by his investment company, he commented, "I have insurance, but no assurance."

Before parting, this gentleman agreed to have lunch with me. The next day, while we dined and talked, he understood at last that salvation is a gift from God, not something he needed to work hard to earn.

Right there in the restaurant, the man bowed his head, opened his heart, and prayed to receive Jesus as Savior. The transformation in his life was instantaneous. He finally had eternal life—and he knew it!

No Greater Thrill

Leading people to Christ is exciting! The miracle of winning someone to faith in Christ surpasses any thrill this world has to offer.

Have you had that experience yet?

If not, I urge you to consider the Lord's Great Commission anew as you continue reading this chapter.

God is calling you to be a Promise Keeper, a man of integrity. You know that. But have you grasped that the Lord is calling you to be a godly man who—as much as anything else—is committed to influencing his family, friends, neighbors, work associates, countrymen, and others around the world for Jesus Christ?

Incredible? Idealistic? Impossible? Listen to what the Lord Jesus said:

> All authority in heaven and on earth has been given to me. Therefore go and make disciples of all nations, baptizing them in the name of the Father and of the Son and of the Holy Spirit, and teaching them to obey everything I have commanded you. And surely I am with you always, to the very end of the age. (Matt. 28:18-20)

"Well, Luis," you may say, "I agree, the Lord does want us to help fulfill His Great Commission in our generation. It's just that, um, I suspect He's thinking more of using you than using me. After all, I certainly don't have the gift of evangelism."

Cut!

I don't see anything in the Great Commission about gifting or talent or ability or personality or even opportunity.

The Lord is clear: "You . . . and you . . . and you, I'm calling all of you men to go, make disciples."

It's not a matter of gift, it's a matter of obedience.

"Lord, I promise to help fulfill Your Great Commission."

Will you?

It's not a matter of gift, it's a matter of heart.

Heart for the World

Thousands of godly men have helped fulfill the Great Commission throughout the world during the closing centuries of this millennium. How can we be like them?

I've studied that question and found the answer has little to do with method or technique. Some have preached before the masses, some in churches. Some have presented the gospel in small groups, mostly one-on-one. Most have used a combination of approaches. But that isn't what made them effective fishers of men.

What I've found is that the great "fishers of men" (Matt. 4:19) over the years all have shared ten distinctives that gave them a tremendous heart for the world. Both Scripture and church history speak to the importance of these distinctives that should shape every Christian man's heart and life:

- passion for those apart from Christ
- Christ-centered message
- holiness in every area of life
- vision to reach the great cities
- boldness to try new methods
- willingness to endure criticism
- commitment to a local church
- love for the whole Body of Christ
- sacrificial financial giving
- seriousness about private prayer
- faithfulness to the end

Sounds like a Promise Keeper, doesn't it?

Unfortunately, today, the first distinctive listed above is sorely missing in our churches. So many lack any measure of concern for those who have not yet trusted Christ as Savior.

How's your heart? How can we sit around while so many press forward all that much closer to an eternity without Christ? For heaven's sake—if nothing else!—we must do something.

Almost all of us get nervous about witnessing. At least I do, even after all these years. But when we willingly obey the Lord, He uses us.

A Willing Heart

Today, before another hour goes by, *let's look to the Lord and say, "Yes, I am willing to help fulfill Your Great Commission."* That's prerequisite to all else.

Unless we're willing to say yes to the Lord in *every* area, there's no use pretending we're a Promise Keeper in *any* area of life, wouldn't you agree?

A Profound Message

Second, *let's begin to take pride in the good news of Jesus Christ*. Like the apostle Paul, let's affirm, "I am not ashamed of the gospel." Why? "Because it is the power of God for the salvation of everyone who believes" (Rom. 1:16).

It's sick what pride the world takes in its debauchery and sin. As Promise Keepers, shouldn't we be all the more proud of the liberating, life-changing gospel of Christ?

What is the gospel? It's "For God so loved the world that he gave his one and only Son, that whoever believes in him shall not perish but have eternal life" (John 3:16).

The gospel is "that Christ died for our sins according to the Scriptures, that he was buried, that he was raised on the third day according to the Scriptures, and that he appeared to Peter, and then to the Twelve," and then to the five hundred (1 Cor. 15:3-6).

It's no more than those great truths, no less. It's simple enough for a child to understand, profound enough to amaze the most brilliant theologians.

Are we proud enough to share this good news with others?

A World of Confusion

Third, *let's gain a better understanding of those outside Christ*. To me, the word that best describes our society today is *confusion*. According to the latest Gallup polls, an astounding eight out of ten Americans claim to be Christians. But ask the average American to define what he or she means and you'll be in for a surprise. Here are some of the most popular myths about what makes someone a Christian:

- thinking positively
- living a good life
- attending church
- giving to others
- receiving a sacrament
- believing in God
- talking about Jesus
- praying

• reading the Bible

Those are all good things, but they're not good enough! Let's take God at His Word and not believe everything men tell us. Just because someone says he is a Christian doesn't mean he's right.

A Message for All Men

Fourth, *let's remember the gospel isn't just for "nice" people*. When God calls us to become Promise Keepers, He is not calling us to shun those whose values, beliefs, and actions are diametrically opposed to ours (see 1 Cor. 5:9-10).

Moments before Westley Allan Dodd was executed by hanging at Washington State Penitentiary in 1993, the convicted serial child killer was given the customary opportunity for last words. Here was a man who had viciously abused and mutilated three young boys, a man who said he'd do it again, a man who said there was no hope he'd ever be released from the hideous darkness within his soul.

His final words came as a shock. "I was wrong when I said there was no hope, no peace," Dodd said from the gallows. "There is hope. There is peace. I have found both in the Lord Jesus Christ."

According to a reporter who witnessed the execution, the father of two of the boys murdered by Dodd "hissed quietly" when Dodd invoked Jesus Christ's name.

No one can fault this father for the hiss of contempt and skepticism. Until the last hours of his life, Dodd had shown no signs of remorse. If we're honest, we Promise Keepers will admit to the same skepticism when we hear that a Dodd or a General Noriega or, 20 years ago, a Charles Colson has turned to Jesus and found forgiveness. Though we proclaim otherwise—"Everyone who calls on the name of the Lord will be saved" (Rom. 10:13)—do we ever act as though the gospel is really only for nice people?

In reality, it's much harder for nice people to find salvation than it is for bad people. C.S. Lewis wrote: "There is even, when you come to think it over, a reason why nasty people might be expected to turn to Christ in greater numbers than nice ones. That was what people objected to about Christ during his life on earth: he seemed to attract 'such awful people.' "

Take Zacchaeus, for example. Jesus' encounter with that tax-gathering cheat was the context for His statement that the "Son of Man came to seek and to save what was lost" (Luke 19:10). When Jesus was invited to the home of Simon the Pharisee, "a woman who had lived a sinful life" wet His feet with her tears, wiped them with her hair, and poured perfume on them. Simon expected Jesus, if He were a prophet, to rebuke this woman of ill repute. Instead, Jesus said to her, "Your sins are forgiven" (Luke 7:37, 48; see 36-48).

Another tax collector, Levi, invited Jesus to a banquet at his home. The Pharisees complained to Jesus' disciples, "Why do you eat and drink with tax collectors and 'sinners'?"

Jesus answered, "It is not the healthy who need a doctor, but the sick. I have not come to call the righteous, but sinners to repentance" (Luke 5:29-32).

Scripture is filled with "who would have thought?" conversions, including a fair number of skeptics. Saul of Tarsus was "a blasphemer and a persecutor and a violent man" (1 Tim. 1:13). Ananias wondered if such a man could ever be changed by grace, let alone overnight. But even "the worst of sinners" was shown mercy. In this context, the apostle Paul could write, "Here is a trustworthy saying that deserves full acceptance: Christ Jesus came into the world to save sinners—of whom I am the worst" (1 Tim. 1:15).

If it seems that grace is being pushed to the limit in rescuing child killers, drug traffickers, and those who vigorously oppose us, we haven't begun to fathom God's ocean of grace and mercy. Nor have we peered long enough into our own hearts.

Years ago, I met a Methodist minister who worked in the inner city of Bristol, England. Asked what he did there, he replied, "I minister to the last, the least, the lonely, and the lost." That was precisely the mission of Jesus.

How often we hear the testimony, "If God can save me, He can save anybody." Yes, He can and does. Together, let's ask God to save the not-so-nice people we meet in our neighborhoods, schools, workplaces, and marketplaces.

A World to Win

Finally, *let's gain a new vision of helping fulfill the Great Commission in our generation.* When you think about those who have never committed their lives to Jesus Christ, who comes to mind? Write down the names of at least five people you'd like to see trust Christ. Begin praying daily for their salvation. Ask God to draw at least one of them to Himself before the end of the year.

Then think about the crowds you see in the cities—at the airports, in the streets, everywhere. How do you feel when you think about them?

Scripture tells us that when Jesus saw the crowds, "he had compassion on them, because they were harassed and helpless, like sheep without a shepherd" (Matt. 9:36). We need to ask God to move our hearts with the same compassion that moves His.

Two of the greatest dangers we face as Promise Keepers are cynicism and a cool detachment: "So more than 3 billion people don't know Christ. That's too bad." We must not forget the actual people—including those we know and love—behind that number who live "without hope and without God in the world" (Eph. 2:12).

The Lord pointed out the urgency of helping fulfill the Great Commission by reminding His disciples, "The harvest is plentiful but the workers are few" (Matt. 9:37). We must sense the urgency of our time. How long must people wait before they hear the gospel? How many more generations must pass before some parts of the world hear the message for the first time?

It's exciting to see the tremendous harvest being reaped in most of the so-called Third World today. Several nations in Latin America, Africa, and Asia could become 51 percent Christian within ten or 15 years. Right now the doors are open as perhaps never before. Mass communications have made it possible to reach even "closed" countries with the message of life. All of this is before us now, but it could pass in such a short time.

Our task is urgent. That's why Jesus commanded His disciples, "Ask the Lord of the harvest, therefore, to send out workers into his harvest field" (Matt. 9:38). Our Bibles end the chapter right there, but don't stop reading! In the next five verses, the Lord gave His disciples authority and sent them out into the harvest. The twelve became an answer to their own prayer!

To finish the task, we must have the authority of God that comes from a holy life. Paul told Timothy, "God did not give us a spirit of timidity, but a spirit of power, of love and of self-discipline" (2 Tim. 1:7). I like to think of that as holy boldness.

The unfinished task of winning the world to Christ is enormous. Are you willing to gain a compassion for the unsaved and a sense of urgency in reaching them for Christ? Are you available to serve God with holy boldness as a Promise Keeper? Let's press on to finish the task set before us.

A Man and His World
Personal Evaluation

1. If you haven't done so already, make a list of everyone you don't like or who has hurt you in the past and you find hard to love. This list should be kept private, for your own spiritual help. Now pray for each person on that list. Can you decide today to love each of them by faith?
2. Are you willing to help fulfill the Great Commission in your world for the glory of God?

    _____ Yes
    _____ No
    _____ I don't know

3. Make a list of people you know who probably do not know Christ. Now begin to pray for their salvation daily.

In the Group

1. Complete the following statement: The reason I find it so hard to love someone who has hurt me is . . . (Each member should do this.)
2. How will you know you are loving someone by faith?
3. Has anyone in the group had the experience of leading someone to faith in Christ? Those who have, tell about one experience and how you felt as that person responded.
4. What are some ways we can reach out to those non-Christians around us—for example, in our work or our neighborhoods?
5. Read silently the epilogue by Coach Bill McCartney. Then look over the list of seven promises of a Promise Keeper. Are you committed to living by them? If not, why not? Talk about what your lives would look like if each of you were. If someone in the group is not ready to make that commitment, be encouraging. Help him pray about it and count the cost.
6. Review the list of seven promises again. Of the seven, which one requires your primary attention now? Tell the group what you plan to do to strengthen that commitment. (Each member should do this.)
7. If the group wishes to continue to meet, further resources listed in the back of the book will allow you to go deeper into each of the promises. You might consider choosing one of those books and working through it for the next eight to 12 weeks.

Memory Verse: "A new command I give you: Love one another. As I have loved you, so you must love one another. By this all men will know that you are my disciples, if you love one another" (John 13:34-35).

Memory Verse: "Then Jesus came to them and said, 'All authority in heaven and on earth has been given to me. Therefore go and make disciples of all nations, baptizing them in the name of the Father and of the Son and of the Holy Spirit, and teaching them to obey everything I have commanded you. And surely I am with you always, to the very end of the age' " (Matt. 28:18-20).

On Your Own

Review the response page in the back of the book. If you're ready to identify yourself as a Promise Keeper, committed to living out the seven promises, sign the page, remove it from the book, and mail it to Promise Keepers. You will then receive a certificate suitable for framing, plus other helpful materials.

Seeking God's Favor

by
Bill McCartney

There's tremendous power in the spoken word. When a man gives you his word, if he's worth his salt, he'll deliver on all he promises. Let me illustrate what I mean.

Back in 1987, our Colorado University football team was preparing to go to Norman, Oklahoma, to play the Sooners. They were the top-ranked team in the country and coming home to play after being on the road. In addition, our C.U. team was extremely young. For as long as anyone could remember, the Sooners had intimidated Colorado not only with their talent, but also with their downright offensive demeanor. Colorado had become a cakewalk for them. They had won 13 of the previous 14 head-to-head matchups and had averaged more than 40 points a game in doing it. Colorado was one of the big reasons Oklahoma was turning out All-Americans and Heisman Trophy winners!

Clearly, we needed to try a new approach. I had to find some way to motivate my players to give the performance of their lives. I finally decided to issue a challenge based on their word as young men. On the Thursday night before the game, I laid this on them: "Men," I said, "no one is getting on that plane for the trip to Norman until he has looked me in the eye and told me what I can expect of him in Saturday's game."

The next morning, I set aside three hours and met individually in my office with the 60 players who would be making the trip. Three minutes each; that's all it took.

As I summoned each young man into my office and had him sit down across from me, I'd look at him and say, "Now, son, I want to know what I can expect from you when we go to Norman to play Oklahoma."

Each one looked me squarely in the eye and said something like, "Coach, you can count on me to play every down to the best of my ability. I'll play my heart out against Oklahoma." Then, depending on his position, each player added, "I'll block better than I've ever blocked before. I'll tackle with more authority. I'll run with precision and strength."

I'd tell each man, "I'm going to hold you to your word," then add that I wanted him to be positive and excited so his teammates would pick up on that attitude.

Having set the tone with those meetings, the team that boarded that plane was on a mission. I knew that collectively, those 60 players would spend themselves in a valiant effort. I didn't know if we could win, but I knew we wouldn't lose because of a lack of effort. Those young men would play their hearts out—and they did.

The game was contested at night and nationally televised on ESPN, so I realized that a lot of the high-school players we were trying to recruit around the country would be watching. And what they saw, before the night was over, was that we would no longer lay down for O.U.! We did, indeed, spend ourselves, trailing by just four points at halftime, though we eventually lost 24-6. But the good news was that each of us knew he had given himself for the team. Each player kept his promise and extended himself. We had taken a significant step forward as a team.

If that kind of dynamic exists in a man's word to a football coach, how much more is it at work when men gather in Jesus' name, look each other squarely in the eyes, and say what can be expected of them? When that happens, there's an unleashing of God's Spirit, an outpouring of His grace and strength that enables us to become Promise Keepers, men who are willing to contend for God's truth.

Now, bear in mind that our ultimate goal—being "conformed to the likeness of his Son" (Rom. 8:29)—is a lifelong process. Just as my Colorado football teams didn't become national contenders overnight, so we won't instantly become perfectly godly men. But just as Colorado football began its transformation into a championship program to a large extent with that one game, so we start by committing our lives to Jesus Christ and becoming a new creation (see 2 Cor. 5:17). Then we make the kinds of commitments to growth embodied in the seven promises covered in this book, and we make them to other men who will hold us accountable and give us the benefit of their experience and wisdom. As we do this, our thoughts, words, decisions, and actions *will change* over time. And our families, friends, co-workers, churches, and communities will receive the blessing of God's work in us.

But there's a lot to chew on in this book, isn't there? Seven areas of commitment, each of them big and potentially life-changing. The task may seem overwhelming. So where do you start? Let me suggest that you prayerfully reflect on what you've read and then identify *the one thing* that God's Spirit has most impressed upon your heart as something you need to do.

Next, take that one thing to a Christian brother, look him in the eyes, and tell him what he can expect from you. When he does the same to you, again look him squarely in the eyes and say, "As your brother in Christ, I'm going to hold you to it." Then encourage each other along the way. Pray for each other; call one another regularly; rally your brother when he's weak. Catch your brother when he falls, and be his biggest fan when he succeeds.

You see, when you make a promise to a brother, you declare your intentions and obligate yourself to follow through. You bind yourself to that person, too. You actually look into the future and determine, by your deliberate choice, that part of it related to your promise.

Jesus said, "Enter through the narrow gate. For wide is the gate and broad is the road that leads to destruction, and many enter through it. But small is the gate and narrow the road that leads to life, and only a few find it" (Matt. 7:13-14). Most men are on the broad road. Which one will you walk?

We're in a war, men, whether we acknowledge it or not. The enemy is real, and he doesn't like to see men of God take a stand for Jesus Christ and contest his lies (see 2 Cor. 10:3-5). But Almighty God is for us, and we know that if we walk the narrow road that leads to life, we have an extremely capable leader in Jesus, the King of kings and Lord of lords. And He is faithful to provide the grace and strength we need along the way.

You and I serve royalty, and we have a costly responsibility. But listen to this promise in John 12:26: "My Father will honor the one who serves me." Accordingly, there's nothing I want more in life than to serve Jesus Christ, because I want Almighty God's favor on me. How about you?

Additional Resources

PROMISE 1

Edwin Louis Cole, *Strong Men in Tough Times* (Orlando: Creation House, 1993).
Charles Colson, *Loving God* (Grand Rapids, Mich.: Zondervan, 1983).
Richard Foster, *Celebration of Discipline* (San Francisco: Harper & Row, 1988).
Jack Hayford, *Worship His Majesty* (Dallas: Word, 1987).
William Carr Peel, *What God Does When Men Pray* (Colorado Springs, Colo.: NavPress, 1993).
Charles R. Swindoll, *Flying Closer to the Flame* (Dallas: Word, 1993).

PROMISE 2

Bobb Biehl, *How to Find a Mentor and How to Become One* (Master Planning Group, P.O. Box 6128, Laguna Niguel, CA 92697; (714) 495-8850).
Geoff Gorsuch and Dan Schaffer, *Brothers! Calling Men into Vital Relationships* (Denver: Promise Keepers, 1993).
James Osterhous, *Bonds of Iron* (Chicago: Moody, 1994).
Peter A. Richardson, *Focusing Your Men's Ministry* (Denver: Promise Keepers, 1993).
David E. Schroeder, *"Follow Me": The Master's Plan for Men* (Grand Rapids, Mich.: Baker, 1992).
Paul D. Stanley and Robert J. Clinton, *Connecting: The Mentoring Relationships You Need to Succeed in Life* (Colorado Springs, Colo.: NavPress, 1992).

PROMISE 3

Tom Eisenman, *Temptations Men Face* (Downers Grove, Ill.: InterVarsity, 1990).
Tony Evans, *Victorious Christian Life* (Nashville: Thomas Nelson, 1994).
Josh McDowell, *Sex, Guilt, and Forgiveness* (San Bernardino, Calif.: Here's Life, 1987).
Gary J. Oliver, *Real Men Have Feelings Too* (Chicago: Moody, 1993).
Doug Sherman and William Hendricks, *Your Work Matters to God* (Colorado Springs, Colo.: NavPress, 1987).

PROMISE 4

Ken R. Canfield, *The 7 Secrets of Effective Fathers* (Wheaton, Ill.: Tyndale, 1992).

Dr. James Dobson, *The New Dare to Discipline* (Wheaton, Ill.: Tyndale, 1992).
Dr. James Dobson, *What Wives Wish Their Husbands Knew About Women* (Wheaton, Ill.: Tyndale, 1977).
Steve Farrar, *Point Man* (Portland, Ore.: Multnomah, 1990).
Gary Smalley, *Joy That Lasts* (Grand Rapids, Mich.: Zondervan, 1986).
Gary Smalley and John Trent, *The Hidden Value of a Man* (Colorado Springs, Colo.: Focus on the Family, 1992).
Charles R. Swindoll, *Strike the Original Match* (Portland, Ore.: Multnomah, 1980).

PROMISE 5

Charles Colson, *The Body* (Dallas: Word, 1992).
Gene A. Getz, *The Measure of a Church* (Glendale, Calif.: Regal, 1975).
Jack Hayford, *The Key to Everything* (Orlando: Creation House, 1993).
H.B. London, Jr., and Neil B. Wiseman, *Pastors at Risk* (Wheaton, Ill.: Victor, 1993).

PROMISE 6

John Perkins, *Let Justice Roll Down* (Ventura, Calif.: Regal, 1976).
Spencer Perkins and Chris Rice, *More Than Equals* (Downers Grove, Ill.: InterVarsity, 1993).
Raleigh Washington and Greg Kehrein, *Breaking Down Walls* (Chicago: Moody, 1993).

PROMISE 7

Joseph C. Aldrich, *Life-Style Evangelism: Crossing Traditional Boundaries to Reach the Unbelieving World* (Portland, Ore.: Multnomah, 1983).
Bill Bright, *Witnessing* (Nashville: Thomas Nelson, 1993).
Robert E. Coleman, *The Master Plan for Evangelism* (Old Tappan, N.J.: Revell, 1963).
Luis Palau, *Say Yes!* (Portland, Ore.: Multnomah, 1991).
Rebecca M. Pippert, *Out of the Saltshaker and into the World* (Downers Grove, Ill.: InterVarsity, 1979).

OTHER BOOKS:

Dr. James C. Dobson, *Straight Talk* (Dallas: Word, 1991).
Gene A. Getz, *The Measure of a Man* (Glendale, Calif.: Regal, 1974)
Robert Hicks, *The Masculine Journey* (Colorado Springs, Colo.: NavPress, 1993).
Bill McCartney, *What Makes a Man?* (Colorado Springs, Colo.: NavPress, 1992).
Patrick Morley, *The Man in the Mirror* (Nashville: Thomas Nelson, 1992).
Stu Weber, *Tender Warrior* (Portland, Ore.: Multnomah, 1993).

If you have chosen to be a Promise Keeper, we would like to know. Please contact us at the address below:

PROMISE KEEPERS
P.O. BOX 18376
Boulder, CO 80308
U.S.A.

PROMISE KEEPERS
MEN OF INTEGRITY

Now that you've read **Seven Promises of a Promise Keeper**, have you decided to live by those seven commitments? Promise Keepers seeks to unite men who understand that becoming a Promise Keeper is a *process*. If you're ready to stand shoulder to shoulder with us, tear out this card along the perforated line and mail it to Promise Keepers. You will receive, free of charge, a wallet-size card and certificate symbolizing your commitment.

1. **A Man and His God:** A Promise Keeper is committed to honoring Jesus Christ through worship, prayer, and obedience to God's Word in the power of the Holy Spirit.
2. **A Man and His Mentors:** A Promise Keeper is committed to pursuing vital relationships with a few other men, understanding that he needs brothers to help him keep his promises.
3. **A Man and His Integrity:** A Promise Keeper is committed to practicing spiritual, moral, ethical, and sexual purity.
4. **A Man and His Family:** A Promise Keeper is committed to building strong marriages and families through love, protection, and biblical values.
5. **A Man and His Church:** A Promise Keeper is committed to supporting the mission of the church by honoring and praying for his pastor, and by actively giving his time and resources.
6. **A Man and His Brothers:** A Promise Keeper is committed to reaching beyond any racial and denominational barriers to demonstrate the power of biblical unity.
7. **A Man and His World:** A Promise Keeper is committed to influencing his world, being obedient to the Great Commandment (see Mark 12:30-31) and the Great Commission (see Matt. 28:19-20).

Yes, I have chosen to become a Promise Keeper and live by these seven commitments.

____

Signed *(Please type or print clearly)*

NAME ______________________________

ADDRESS ______________________________

CITY ________________ STATE ________ COUNTRY ________

DAYTIME PHONE: ______ (COUNTRY CODE) ______ (CITY CODE) ______ (NUMBER) EVENING ______ (COUNTRY CODE) ______ (CITY CODE) ______ (NUMBER)

FAX: ______ (COUNTRY CODE) ______ (CITY CODE) ______ (NUMBER)

Detach, enclose in envelope and mail to Promise Keepers at the address provided.

Code 120

Promise Keepers
P.O. Box 18376
Boulder, CO 80308
U.S.A.